The Junior High School

THE LIBRARY OF EDUCATION

A Project of The Center for Applied Research in Education, Inc.

G. R. Gottschalk, Director

Categories of Coverage

I	II	III
Curriculum and Teaching	Administration, Organization, and Finance	Psychology for Educators

IV	V	VI
History, Philosophy, and Social Foundations	Professional Skills	Educational Institutions

The Junior High School

R. P. BRIMM

Principal, State College High School
and
Professor of Teaching
State College of Iowa

41992

The Center for Applied Research in Education, Inc.
New York

Second printing.......August, 1964

LIBRARY OF CONGRESS
CATALOG CARD NO.: 63–13296

PRINTED IN THE UNITED STATES OF AMERICA

Foreword

During the last two decades the American junior high school movement has achieved new and, in certain aspects, amazing dimensions. To the casual observer, the most remarkable recent changes in this movement are the large increase in the number of junior high schools, the enormous growth of enrollment, and the resulting expansion of the professional staff. Quite as extraordinary, however, and to the critical observer even more significant, has been the recent heartening increase in attention and serious study now being devoted to the junior high school by thoughtful students of secondary education. This growing concern is demonstrated by the current research bearing on the junior high school, by the constantly growing body of useful professional literature dealing with it, and by the increasing number of courses, workshops, and conferences devoted to serious consideration of its problems.

Happily, much of the writing in this professional area is now being done by individuals who are conversant with the theoretical aspects of the movement and, in addition, are competent, practicing principals and teachers who are actively testing their theories in the junior high schools in their charge.

It is from precisely such a background that Dr. R. P. Brimm prepared this monograph. As a junior high school teacher, a junior high school principal, a superintendent responsible for the administration and supervision of a junior high school program, and currently as the principal of a six-year high school primarily concerned with teacher preparation, Dr. Brimm has had exceptional opportunities for study, observation, and experience. The result is a stimulating, informative, well-organized monograph. It should be extremely useful to all individuals working directly in this field and to others who desire to be brought up-to-date on the junior high school.

JOHN RUFI
Professor Emeritus
University of Missouri

v

Contents

The Junior High School

CHAPTER I

The Junior High School in
the American Educational System

Even before the twelve-grade American public school system was universally adopted, measures were under way to change the pattern. Three new divisions gradually worked their ways into the existing structure. The kindergarten came first and was attached as a lower rung of the educational ladder. It has gradually become an integral part of our public school system. Next, the two-year junior college was superimposed on the top of the educational ladder. The place of the junior college is still undefined; some look upon it as a part of higher education while others accept it as an extension of the secondary school. The third new division to work its way into the structure was the junior high school. It was not attached to the existing system but carved out of the middle. Slowly it has found its position in the pattern of American education.

Although combining the upper portions of the elementary school and the lower portion of the high school, many junior high schools have lost their identity with either of the two schools. In its original conception it was a downward extension of the secondary school rather than an upward expansion of the elementary. Today we find some junior high schools administered by the elementary principal, some administered by the high school principal, and others administered as separate units.

Actually, the junior high school had its beginnings in dissatisfaction with the elementary school program. In the latter part of the nineteenth century, Charles W. Eliot, president of Harvard, argued that the elementary school program should be enriched and shortened. He claimed that much of the upper elementary school program was a review of materials covered earlier. He believed that this time could be better spent in the study of new materials. During the 1890's, he became chairman of the Committee of Ten, which recom-

1

mended a revision of the elementary school. About the same time, the Committee of Fifteen, made up largely of superintendents of large-city school systems, was hesitant about shortening the elementary program but did recommend beginning some high school courses earlier. The recommendations of this committee did not provide for the creation of a separate junior high school.

Shortly after the reports of the Committee of Ten and the Committee of Fifteen appeared, a Committee on College Entrance Requirements was formed by the National Education Association. In 1899, after four years of study, this group recommended a six-year high school. Thus, the recommendation was to change the existing 8–4 system to a 6–6 plan. Around 1910, the "intermediate school" began to appear in some of the larger cities. In some cases it was merely a matter of administrative expediency—setting aside a building to house the upper elementary school—rather than the creation of a new type of school.

The administrative split of 6–2–4 and, in some cases, 6–3–3, gradually set the stage for a reorganization of the program itself. Once the school was housed in separate facilities and administered independently, there was more of an opportunity to break away from the traditional program.

It was not until 1915 that the ninth-grade classes were added to the intermediate school and departmentalization began to replace the self-contained classroom of Grades 7 and 8. Today there is a wide variety of administrative organizations, and varying degrees of departmentalization exist. But, there is a very distinct trend toward the separate junior high school, comprised of Grades 7, 8, and 9, with the same degree of departmentalization that exists in the senior high school. The 6–3–3 organization is more prominent in larger communities while the smaller communities seem to favor the 6–2–4 or 6–6 plan. The most recent figures from the U.S. Office of Education reveal that both in numbers of administrative units and in numbers of pupils served, the 6–6 plan is the more popular.

The Junior High School: Yesterday and Today

In the early planning stages, the concepts of the junior high school were varied and controversial. Some recommendations were based on the idea of merely moving some of the traditional secondary subjects into the upper elementary school. Other recommendations were based on a dissatisfaction with the existing eight-year elementary program. Still others wished to speed up the educational processes so the college-bound pupil could begin his college preparation earlier and possibly be ready to enter college at an earlier age. As time has passed, many arguments have been used to justify the existence of a separate school. Among these have been the reduction of dropouts that were occurring particularly at the end of the eighth grade. At times the vocational function of the junior high has been stressed, but at present the trend seems to be to delay specialized vocational selection and training until later.

Many lists appear in current literature giving the functions of the junior high school. The most commonly quoted list, compiled by Gruhn and Douglass, includes the following items:[1]

1. Integration.
2. Exploration.
3. Guidance.
4. Differentiation.
5. Socialization.
6. Articulation.

A careful study of those functions would probably raise questions as to whether they are unique to the junior high school or equally applicable to other segments of our educational system. It is true that most lists of general objectives may be used to express the program of various levels of our educational system. For example, *Cardinal Principles of Education*[2] was developed by the Commission on the Reorganization of Secondary Education but has been used broadly to express the objectives of education at various grade levels.

The Educational Policies Commission's *Education for all American Youth* prompted a Committee of the National Association of Secondary School Principals to draw up the "Imperative Needs of

[1] William T. Gruhn and Harl R. Douglass, *The Modern Junior High School*, 2nd ed. (New York: The Ronald Press Company, 1956), pp. 31–32.

[2] Commission on the Reorganization of Secondary Education, *Cardinal Principles of Education*, Bulletin 1918, No. 35 (Washington, D.C.: Department of the Interior, Bureau of Education, 1918), pp. 12–13.

Youth."[3] A group of California junior high school administrators modified these general statements to apply more specifically to the early adolescent age. Their "Ten Imperative Needs of Junior High School Youth" are:[4]

1. All junior high school youth need to explore their own aptitudes and to have experiences basic to occupational proficiency.
2. All junior high school youth need to develop and maintain abundant physical and mental health.
3. All junior high school youth need to be participating citizens of their school and community, with increasing orientation to adult citizenship.
4. All junior high school youth need experiences and understandings, appropriate to their age and development, which are the foundation of home and family life.
5. All junior high school youth need to develop a sense of values of material things and of the rights of ownership.
6. All junior high school youth need to learn about the natural and physical environment and its effect on life, and to have opportunities for using the scientific approach in the solution of problems.
7. All junior high school youth need the enriched living which comes from appreciation of and expression in the arts, and from experiencing the beauty and wonder of the world around them.
8. All junior high school youth need to have a variety of socially acceptable and personally satisfying leisure-time experiences which contribute either to their personal growth or to their development in wholesome group relationships, or to both.
9. All junior high school youth need experiences in group living which contribute to personality and character development; they need to develop a respect for other persons and their rights, and to grow in ethical insights.
10. All junior high school youth need to grow in their ability to observe, listen, read, think, speak, and write with purpose and appreciation.

In view of the general nature of these statements of functions and objectives, it must be assumed that such statements cannot be confined to the junior high school. Many could be applied to the elementary school and to the senior high school as well, but their

---

[3] National Association of Secondary School Principals, *Planning for American Youth* (Washington, D.C.: National Association of Secondary School Principals, 1944), p. 43.

[4] Helen Jewett Rogers, "The Emerging Curriculum of the Modern Junior High School," *Bulletin of the National Association of Secondary School Principals,* Vol. 34, No. 170 (April, 1950), 128–29.

implementation is different for the junior high than for other levels of our school system.

Administrative Organization

The administrative organization of the American school system is varied and, on the surface, appears very complex. The fact that we have fifty independent systems administered by states adds to the confusion. Foreign visitors in our country, however, are often very much surprised to find that the systems found in the various states have more similarities than differences. For example, a boy may transfer from the ninth grade of a three-year junior high school in California to the ninth grade of a four-year senior high school in Illinois and find that he can fit into about the same pattern of courses with approximately the same content. Actually, we often find as much variation among the schools in the same state as between two schools in different states.

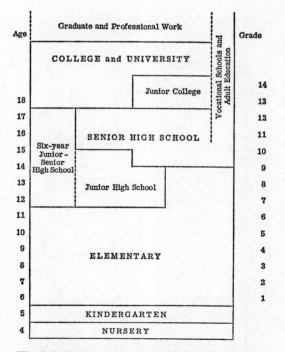

Fig. 1–1. Types of Administrative Organizations.

Figure 1–1 represents some of the different types of administrative organizations found in the United States. But the instructional programs for these various types of schools are not necessarily different. For the most part the differences are merely administrative.

Unlike the European system, the system in the United States permits the transfer of a pupil from one type of school to another. Entrance from a lower school to the next higher one is seldom based on comprehensive examinations. The flow of pupils from one school to another is determined by the local school, where a pupil is "passed" or "retained," in accordance with local policies. In case of transfer from one school to another, grade placement is usually based on the recommendation of the school from which the pupil transfers.

In Fig. 1–1, we see the four most common patterns of 6–6, 6–3–3, 6–2–4, and 8–4 organizations with provisions to transfer from one pattern to another with a minimum of difficulty.

The fastest growing type of organization is the junior-senior high school, followed by the separate three-year junior high school. The growth of the administrative organizations since 1920 is shown by statistics from the U.S. Office of Education.[5]

TABLE 1–1

NUMBER OF PUBLIC SECONDARY SCHOOLS BY TYPE
1920–1959

	1919–20		1951–52		1958–59	
	No.	%	No.	%	No.	%
Combined Junior-Senior High Schools (6–6)	828	5.8	8,591	36.2	10,130	41.9
Separate Junior-Senior High Schools	55	.4	3,227	13.6	4,996	20.6
Senior High Schools (6–3–3)	15	.1	1,021	4.3	1,642	6.8
Reorganized 4-year High Schools (6–2–4)	7	.01	739	3.1	1,396	5.8
Unreorganized 4-year Traditional (8–4)	13,421	93.7	10,168	42.8	6,023	24.9
Total	14,326	100.0	23,746	100.0	24,187	100.0

Not only is the 6–6 organization most common in terms of the number of administrative units but this plan enrolls more pupils than

[5] National Association of Secondary School Principals, *News Letter,* Vol. 8, No. 5 (May–June, 1961).

any other type. In Table 1–2 it will be noted that the junior-senior, separate junior, and separate senior high schools enroll over 70 per cent of students in all types of secondary schools.[6]

Two other plans for reorganization have been suggested. Although these have attracted some attention, very little has been done to

TABLE 1–2

ENROLLMENTS BY TYPE OF ORGANIZATION
1920–1959

	1919–20		1951–52		1958–59	
	No.	%	No.	%	No.	%
Combined Junior-Senior High Schools (6–6)	276,504	13.8	2,696,707	35.1	3,536,921	32.0
Separate Junior-Senior High School	37,331	1.9	1,526,996	19.8	2,749,602	24.9
Senior High School (6–3–3)	11,994	.6	868,848	11.3	1,624,713	14.7
Reorganized 4-year High School (6–2–4)	5,797	.3	659,158	8.6	1,193,518	10.8
Unreorganized 4-year Traditional (8–4)	1,667,480	83.4	1,937,210	25.2	1,939,365	17.6
Total	1,999,106	100.0	7,688,919	100.0	11,044,119	100.0

place them in actual operation. The first, suggested by Koos,[7] is a plan to extend the junior high school to four years, followed by another four-year organization that would bring the last two years of the senior high school and the junior college into one administrative unit. This 6–4–4 plan is claimed to have advantages for the junior high school in that it would provide for an extra year in developing a curriculum of greater enrichment and expanded possibilities in exploration. Another advantage would be that it would capitalize upon the greater maturity of the pupils for leadership in various aspects of both class and extraclass programs.

---

[6] *Ibid.,* 4.
[7] Leonard V. Koos, *Integrating High School and College: The Six-Four-Four Plan At Work* (New York: Harper & Row, Publishers, 1946).

The second plan, offered by Woodring,[8] is often referred to as a 4–4–4–4 organization. Actually this plan is not intended to set up a fixed pattern, but instead moves the pupil through various educational sequences at different rates of speed. The program would start with an ungraded primary school for children of about five. The number of years spent in this school would vary from two to five, depending upon the development and progress of the child. The primary school would be followed by a "middle school" of four to five years, and then by the high school. The high school would be terminal for the less able at about sixteen, while the others would go on to junior colleges and trade schools. The more able would enter the liberal arts college at an earlier age and then go on to the university and professional schools for specialization.

The Unique Functions of the Junior High School

Long lists of purposes of the junior high school have appeared in professional literature but in the final analysis all of these must be based upon one single function—the provision of an educational program for the early adolescent years. Thus the primary function of this administrative unit of our school system is to meet the physical, social, emotional, and intellectual characteristics of the particular age group it serves. The guidance function is important at all levels, but the guidance services of the junior high school must be different from those of the elementary school or the senior high school if they are to be effective. By the same token, exploration and socialization are found at all educational levels but the junior high schools must design these portions of their programs to be meaningful to the particular age group served.

It is of utmost importance that teachers and administrators who work with the early adolescent youth understand some of the problems that are peculiar to this particular group. Physical, social, and intellectual maturity exists in varying degrees among the boys and girls of this age. Some early adolescent children have grown rapidly; others have not. Those who have reached the physical size of an adult have not attained the physical maturity of adulthood. The differences between social and emotional maturity, so evident among

---

[8] Paul Woodring, *A Fourth of a Nation* (New York: McGraw-Hill Book Co., Inc., 1957), p. 147.

various members of the age group, are also present within a single individual. This is well illustrated by the junior high school girl dressed in formal attire and amusing herself with a yo-yo and bubble gum while waiting for her date to take her to the spring formal. The child who often looks and acts like an adult still has desires to participate in the activities of the young child. The dolls and other playthings of the early adolescent still have a place of prominence in the closet filled with high heels and smartly tailored adult-type clothing. This is an age of transition, and in this transition elements of the old and of the new are necessary.

Thus the unique functions of the junior high school may be expressed in a program that provides for a transition from the total life of the pre-adolescent to the new life of the young adult. The functions may be expressed as follows:

1. Transition from the self-contained classroom of the elementary school to the highly departmentalized classes of the senior high school.

2. Transition from the emphasis on the basic skills of the elementary school to the content courses of the senior high school.

3. Transition from the program of all required courses of the elementary school to the elective program of the senior high school.

4. Transition from the childhood activities of the pre-adolescent to the accepted adult activities of the young adult.

5. Transition from the pre-adolescent set of values to the more serious adult values of our modern, complex economy.

6. Transition from the social patterns of childhood to the social life of the adult which draws a definite distinction between the activities of the sexes.

The school system that ignores these transitional functions of the junior high school has little justification for a separate administrative unit.

Conant's[9] investigation of the junior high school shows too many schools ignoring the real functions of the junior high school and actually operating a "little high school" patterned after the senior high school. Such a plan violates the basic principles of the junior high school and serves no real purpose in our educational program. The highly departmentalized content courses of the junior high school do not provide for a transition period. Instead, it "dumps" the

[9] James B. Conant, *Education In the Junior High School Years* (Princeton, N.J.: Educational Testing Service, 1960).

seventh-grader into a new situation two years earlier than did the unreorganized 8–4 plan, when he is less able to cope with the new situation.

The elementary school child cannot change over to the patterns of older youth overnight. The school that does not provide for a transition period is violating one of the basic principles of psychology and cannot expect effective results from its educational program.

CHAPTER II

The Psychological Basis
for the Junior High School

There is a common fallacy in the thinking of many persons as to the psychological justification for the separate junior high school. The neat classification of the elementary school for the pre-adolescent, the junior high school for the early adolescent, and the senior high school for the middle adolescent is very convenient, but cannot be supported by practice. Even a superficial look at any group of junior high school pupils will immediately point out wide discrepancies in this classification.

The junior high school normally enrolls pupils within the twelve-fifteen age range. Even though there may be a fair degree of homogeneity in age, there are many other factors that cause a wide range of differences. The most noticeable differences are between the pupils of different sexes. Cole[1] points out that, on the average, girls achieve early adolescence from ages eleven to thirteen years; boys from fifteen to seventeen years. Thus a girl of thirteen or fourteen years of age may be in the late adolescent period of development while a boy of the same age may be in the pre-adolescent period. Even among children of the same sex there is often a wide range of difference in maturity at the junior high school level.

The wide range of maturity in physical, psychological, mental, emotional, and sexual traits make it all but impossible to establish a system that would homogeneously group early adolescents into a unique school designed specifically to meet the exact needs of various maturity levels. Thus, to understand the junior high school pupil, it is necessary to understand the psychology of the boys and girls as they progress from late childhood into late adolescence. Many factors seem to affect maturity levels to some degree. Some of these are race, family, climate, nutrition, and health. These external

---

[1] Luella Cole, *Psychology of Adolescence,* 5th ed. (New York: Holt, Rinehart & Winston, Inc., 1959), p. 4.

factors and many others cause complications in establishing a junior high school to serve a specific group.

Frank and Frank[2] point out that many problems of the adolescent stem from sexual maturation. This phase of maturation causes physical disturbances that are strange and the youth becomes guarded and secretive about them. At this stage the boys and girls begin to recognize the reasons behind some of the adult social conventions, yet they are unsure of themselves in proper social situations.

The physical changes of development are often sources of embarrassment to the youth and various defensive mechanisms are developed. In addition to the physical changes there are new social situations that he recognizes but is unsure of his ability to cope with. His pre-adolescent accomplishments are not sufficient to win recognition in the new society and he often resorts to socially unacceptable activities to gain recognition. Social acceptance by his peers seems more important to him than adult acceptance and as a result his progress toward adult social standards is often delayed.

As far as psychologists have been able to establish, there are no differences between the learning processes of the adolescent and those of older or younger individuals. At one time it was thought that learning capabilities were stronger during the early teen-age period and slowed down as the person attained maturity. Recent research indicates that man's capabilities develop well into the adult years. There is evidence to support the principle that physical and mental development are related. It seems generally true that the child who matures physically at an early age normally matures mentally at an early age. This would indicate that we could expect to find a wide range of mental maturity between children at different stages of physical maturity.

The entire picture of the junior high school pupil is very complex. The situation is well summarized by Gruhn's statement: "Psychologists seem agreed that the predominate characteristic of early adolescents is that at no other age are children so different from each other."[3] Such a situation demands a wide variation in teaching techniques if it is to be handled in an effective manner.

---

[2] Lawrence K. Frank and Mary Frank, *Your Adolescent At Home and in the School* (New York: The Viking Press, Inc., 1956), p. 60.

[3] William T. Gruhn, "Reaffirming the Role of the Junior High School in the American School System," *Bulletin of the National Association of Secondary School Principals,* Vol. 44, No. 259 (November, 1960), 7.

Psychological differences in the adolescent may be traced to causes ranging from biological to social. Regardless of the origin of the differences, the realistic approach is the acceptance of the fact that there is a wide range of differences and that the school must cope with them. The teacher must realize the variety of differences and be able to recognize and deal with them.

Even a cursory survey of the findings in the field of adolescent psychology will reveal that the commonly stated functions of the junior high school are based upon sound psychological principles. The transitional function is evident as there is a wide variation in both the degree and rate of physical and sexual maturity. As the child enters into this stage of change in his life, there are many other changes precipitated by changing biological factors. As he matures, his position in society changes and new and strange demands are placed upon him. These demands require radical changes in his social adjustments that very often cause emotional disturbances. The solutions of these multiplying problems must be faced by the school. Faunce and Clute[4] offer the solution that "Much depends on how well his teachers understand the problems and how well they are able to organize teaching and learning activities."

As we will see in later chapters, the organization of the junior high school is largely in the areas of common learnings in which most of the pupils are placed in the same classes. If this means that all the pupils, with this wide range of differences, are to be submitted to the same experiences, we are likely to meet with a major disaster. We can expect a wider range of individual differences in the junior high school than in any other division of our school system. No administrative device such as grade placement, age placement, or ability grouping can do the job adequately. Certain devices may reduce the range of differences to a limited degree but in the final analysis the teacher must provide for individual differences in each classroom. Here lies the major challenge to the junior high school organization and to the administrators and teachers who operate it.

Although transition seems to be the factor of major concern, all the forces of guidance must be brought into play and the exploratory function of the school must provide a wide range of varied

---

[4] Roland C. Faunce and Morrell J. Clute, *Teaching and Learning in the Junior High School* (Belmont, Calif.: Wadsworth Publishing Co., Inc., 1961), pp. 48–49.

activities to meet the needs of these boys and girls. The school that can successfully help boys and girls in this period of change is the junior high school which is organized and directed as a school for the transitional period.

CHAPTER III

The Instructional Program

Early ideas for the junior high school envisioned moving the traditional senior high school courses into the seventh and eighth grades. This was suggested so that college preparatory courses could be started earlier and thus speed the capable college-bound student toward an early admission to college. This college-preparatory function of the junior high school was dropped in the early stages of the school and the junior high school's lack of concern with college is often pointed to as one of its strengths. Many administrators feel that the primary function of the junior high school is not to prepare for the requirements of the senior high school and college but to develop a program to meet the needs of the individual.[1] The curriculum developed for the needs of the individual pupil affords much more flexibility than one dictated by the schools higher on the educational ladder.

The practice of pushing senior high school subjects downward into the junior high school seems to have been renewed as a result of the "Sputnik" drive toward science and mathematics in our schools. However, there is a more sensible approach to the problem now than there was in the initial push in this direction. Although some schools have moved entire courses downward, other schools have reorganized the total curriculum so that certain elements of traditional subjects of the senior high school have been placed in the junior high school program. This provides for earlier experiences but does not move a total senior high school course to a lower level without adjustments.

Organization for Instruction

The administrative organization for instruction places limitations upon any school program. Therefore it is essential that any organi-

---

[1] James E. Albrecht and Fred Roessel, "Supervising Guidance Services in Junior High Schools," *Bulletin of the National Association of Secondary School Principals*, Vol. 45, No. 266 (September, 1961), 37.

zation for instruction in a school be so structured that the restrictions do not hinder the objectives for which the school is designed. One of the primary objectives of the junior high school is to provide for a transition from the self-contained classroom of the elementary school to the highly departmentalized program of the senior high school. The organized plan that calls for complete departmentalization in the junior high school is therefore in direct opposition with one of the basic foundations upon which the school is built. This is not a new violation in the basic principles of junior high school organization. Briggs pointed out, as early as 1920, that if sudden departmentalization at the ninth-grade level is bad, then it is worse at the seventh-grade level.[2]

The Carnegie Unit of the senior high school is another organizational device that has been adopted by many junior high schools and has placed serious limitations on instructional programs. The system of the Carnegie Unit was imposed on the secondary school by higher education and has been universally adopted, even though it has restricted flexibility in the program. The junior high school is not under the pressure of colleges, yet this device has been adopted as the junior high school has gradually developed into a "little high school" and the organizational pattern for instruction has been taken from the blue print of the senior high school.

One of the more common practices in organizing the junior high school program for the transitional function is the "block of time" schedule. In 1956 the National Association of Secondary School Principals reported that one of their studies showed that 57.3 per cent of the junior high schools surveyed used a plan for a "block of time" consisting of two or more periods under the same teacher.[3] Other studies have shown that up to 71 per cent of these programs are combinations of English and social studies.[4]

The trend in the junior high school has definitely been in the direction of grouping traditional subjects for instruction. Such traditional elementary subjects as spelling, reading, and composition have been grouped to form a total English program under one teacher, or broadened even further into the language arts concept that encompasses the total field of communications. The social

---

[2] Thomas H. Briggs, *The Junior High School* (Boston: Houghton Mifflin Company, 1920), p. 149.

[3] Roland C. Faunce and Nelson L. Bossing, *Developing the Core Curriculum*, 2nd ed. (Englewood Cliffs, N.J.: Prentice-Hall, Inc., 1958), p. 69.

[4] Faunce and Clute, *op. cit.*, p. 68.

studies concept has tended to place geography, history, and government together. This grouping of subjects into broader fields has not been confined to the traditional subjects of the elementary school; it has also been used in a reorganization of the traditional secondary subjects for the junior high school. Generalized courses, such as general science and general mathematics, have been introduced to provide for the exploratory function and also to bring certain of the traditional senior high school subject matter into the junior high school.

A study of the course offerings in the junior high school will show three different stages. These are:

1. The "segmented" or "piecemeal" program devoting fifteen or twenty minutes to each of twelve or fifteen different subjects such as reading, spelling, penmanship, grammar, history, geography, civics, and so on.

2. The "general" program that has combined the segmented courses in subject matter fields into broader courses.

3. The move toward the "block of time" courses which increases the time allotment for a single teacher and brings two or more subject matter areas within her instructional scope.

The administrative organization for instruction must be determined by the individual school in light of its own facilities and instructional staff. Complete departmentalization starting at the seventh grade may be justifiable if the staff is not properly trained to handle work in more than one field. The "block of time" approach has a very sound guidance basis but this must be weighed against the depth of meaningful instruction in any particular school.

Two examples of seventh-grade programs in two different schools will illustrate the wide range of organizational patterns found in junior high schools.

School A

8:35– 9:25	English—Spelling
9:27–10:17	Literature—Penmanship
10:19–11:09	Art (Thurs.)
	Music (Mon., Wed.)
	Study Hall (Tues. and Fri.)
11:10–12:00	Physical Education (Mon., Wed.)
	Homeroom (Tues., Thurs., Fri.)
12:45– 1:38	Geography
1:40– 2:33	Mathematics
2:35– 3:30	History

(The preceding schedule is of a reorganized school but still carries many of the elements of the traditional segmented elementary program.)

School B

8:00– 9:55	Social Studies—Language Arts
10:00–10:55	Music
	Instrumental (Mon., Wed., Fri.)
	Vocal (Tues., Thurs.)
11:00–11:55	Mathematics
12:40– 1:35	Science
1:40– 2:35	Exploratory Program
	9 weeks—Typewriting
	9 weeks—Home Economics
	9 weeks—Industrial Arts
	9 weeks—Art
2:40– 3:35	Physical Education

These examples present two distinct types of organization. Neither could be declared superior to the other on the basis of the organization. The quality of instruction is influenced to some degree by the administrative organization, but in the final analysis the important elements are the content of the courses and the ability of the teachers.

Language arts. The language arts concept in organization for instruction includes all of the communication skills. In broad areas these are broken down into four major subdivisions: reading, writing, speaking, and listening. Rather than being divided into special courses for the separate areas, they are combined and all areas are stressed in the single course. This type of program is in contrast with the organization that provides a specific time for reading with other periods designated for grammar and other periods set aside for spelling, literature, speech, and composition activities. The segmented plan too often structures a program in which such skills as grammar and spelling are presented in isolation from speaking and writing activities.

Conant's report on the junior high school stresses the importance of continuing the skills program of the elementary school.[4] Concern over the basic communications skills has prompted some schools to maintain their segmented approach to insure that each skill is given

---

[4] James B. Conant, *Education in the Junior High School Years* (Princeton, N.J.: Educational Testing Service, 1960), pp. 20–21.

proper time consideration in the instructional program. Such a plan reflects the administrator's lack of confidence in the teacher's ability to give adequate instruction in all the skills that are so important for adequate communications competency. The broad language arts concept has proven successful in many schools but, like any other program, its success is dependent upon competent teachers. It is questionable that the incompetent teacher will give adequate instruction in all of the language skills even though the administration organization requires a set amount of time to be devoted to each of the skill areas.

Although grammar and usage are aimed at developing competency in speaking and writing, there is evidence to show that these skills are taught in isolation from their actual application. Studies of the time devoted to the various areas of English instruction in public schools were made by Pooley and Roberts[5] in 1945 and by Farmer and Freeman[6] in 1952. Both studies show that much more time was devoted to formal instruction in grammar than to its actual application in writing and speaking.

There has long been a controversy among English teachers as to the merits of formalized grammar drill which includes such activities as diagramming sentences, declining verbs, memorizing definitions for the parts of speech, and memorizing rules. Although a high percentage of leaders in the field urge more stressing understanding and clear expression rather than rules, this is not a widespread practice. The National Council of English[7] has suggested that the standardization of English through rigid rules be avoided and that the students be led to generalize through extensive experiences in writing and thus learn through these experiences rather than through memorization of rules and definitions. However, teachers in general find it difficult to operate a program of usage instruction based upon such flexible criteria. In the final analysis, both the administration and the teacher must realize that real instruction in the classroom cannot be forced through rigid time allotments. Such a plan may serve as a

---

[5] Robert C. Pooley and Robert D. Roberts, *The Teaching of English in Wisconsin* (Madison, Wisc.: University of Wisconsin, 1948).

[6] Paul Farmer and Bernice Freeman, *The Teaching of English in Georgia* (Atlanta: Georgia Council of Teachers of English, 1952).

[7] National Council of English, Commission on the English Curriculum, *The English Language Arts in the Secondary School* (New York: Appleton-Century-Crofts, 1956).

safeguard against the poor teacher but it places restrictions on the good teacher. Authoritative sources continuously recommend more actual writing and speaking practice with the teacher making critical analysis of the work. The problem will be better solved through more flexible time tables and smaller classes in which the teacher can give individual attention to the pupils and provide more actual experiences in writing and speaking.

Reading seems to be one of the major problems in the junior high school today. Conant[8] recommends that every pupil (except the mentally deficient) should read at least at the sixth-grade level by the end of Grade 9. Such an undertaking requires a plan that will include both a reading improvement program for all pupils and a remedial program for those who require it. Although the language arts classes should not carry the full responsibility for a complete reading program, in reality the major load does fall on this phase of instruction. All language arts, including reading, should be a joint responsibility of all subject matter areas but in actual practice social studies, science, mathematics, and other areas look to the language arts program to develop the communication skills. This has been a long-standing problem in the English field but little has been done to convince other subject matter area teachers to hold high standards for their written reports and in the reading level requirements. Science teachers, for instance, are usually more interested in the content of papers than in clarity of expression. Social studies teachers continue to assign common reading materials for eighth-graders at the eighth-grade reading level, regardless of the individual's ability to read the materials.

The old cliché that "every teacher is an English teacher" is verbally accepted in all circles but is not carried through in practice. If high standards and achievement are to be developed in the communications skills, this "cliché" must become a working principle in the junior high school.

The speaking and listening skills of communication are also not the sole responsibility of the language arts programs. Again, these are skills that can best be achieved by holding high standards in all courses of instruction in the school.

Mathematics. Perhaps no phase of the secondary curriculum is

---

8 Conant, *op. cit.,* p. 20.

facing more drastic changes than mathematics. The so-called modern mathematics has developed rapidly during the past few years and, in all probability, will dominate mathematics instruction in the future. Seldom do we find a movement that deviates drastically from the traditional pattern yet is supported both by educators and by "pure" subject matter specialists. However, this appears to be the situation in mathematics.

This new concept in the teaching of mathematics faces two major obstacles: the classroom teacher and the materials of instruction. Both are serious obstacles and can only be overcome through a continuous drive by those leaders who recognize the merits of the program. Teachers who have been adhering to the traditional sequence of mathematics find that a major changeover in their teaching methods will be necessary to follow the new plan. At the same time, few textbook materials are available to assist the teacher in her changeover. The materials that are available are largely in experimental form and a full sequence of mathematics experiences from the elementary school through the senior high school is not yet to be had.

Basically, the two major changes in the modern mathematics approach are:

1. A breakdown in the artificial divisions between arithmetic, algebra, geometry, trigonometry, and other branches of mathematics.

2. Stress on understandings of mathematical concepts rather than on the memorization of formulas and the manipulation of numbers according to established rules.

Although the new mathematics instruction had its start in the senior high school, it has found its most fertile field in the junior high school. The concept of the new generalized approach fits into the exploratory concept of the junior high school very well.

The traditional program of mathematics carried arithmetic through Grade 8 and then went into the algebra, geometry, trigonometry sequence in Grades 9, 10, and 11. A problem met at the eighth-grade level had to be solved by arithmetic yet the same problem at the ninth-grade level required algebra and the mathematical process of solution was altogether different. The modern mathematics approach is to introduce the simpler algebraic and geometric concepts at a lower level and to use the concept that leads to the better way of solving the problem. The various areas of mathematics are closely related but the artificial divisions have kept them apart. The present trend seems to be toward unifying mathematics into a related whole rather than keeping it in unrelated segments.

Algebra has long been a traditional ninth-grade course. As the schools became less selective, however, it was found that the abstractions of algebra became more and more difficult for the less academic student. As a step to correct this situation, the dual track of mathematics became popular. The better student continued to enroll in algebra while the poorer student was placed in a watered-down course of "higher arithmetic," "practical mathematics," or "general mathematics."

The "general" mathematics concept seems to be one of the basic ideas behind the new movement. However, the new movement does not provide a watered-down course for slow ninth-graders. Instead, it introduces a high-level sequence of courses for Grades 7, 8, and 9. The sequence of courses under this plan covers the entire field of mathematics. Algebraic, geometric, and trigonometric concepts are taught at all three grade levels. These concepts are not isolated into separate areas but are fused into a single mathematical whole. This approach serves not only to introduce the junior high school pupil to higher mathematics at an early age, but it also serves the exploratory function of acquainting the pupil with the content of the more specialized courses that he will encounter at the senior high school and college levels.

Social studies.   The term *social studies* as applied to the curriculum of the junior high school differs from the term *social science* as used in the terminology of higher education. The social sciences are advanced and scholarly studies of human relationships based upon experimentation and research. The results of such studies are intended to add to the knowledge and understanding of man in his various relationships. The social studies, on the other hand, are the reorganized and simplified findings of the social sciences.

The Library of Congress lists the following under the classification of the social studies: (1) anthropology, (2) economics, (3) education, (4) geography, (5) history, (6) law, (7) political science, (8) regionalism, and (9) sociology. In addition to these, psychology, criminology, and philosophy are often considered part of this classification. Prior to World War I, the separate courses of history, civics (government), and geography dominated this area in the school curriculum. Between the two world wars, the social studies movement gained ground and gradually became the dominant pattern for instruction. Although history and government still play the prominent role in the junior high school, other phases of the social studies have found their ways into the courses.

There does not seem to be a dominant pattern in today's junior high school social studies organization. Grades 7 and 8 usually have social studies requirements and one of the two years is devoted to American history. A variety of courses is found in the ninth grade, but very often schools do not offer any social studies work at this grade level. The teaching of geography as a separate course is declining; geography is now usually considered in the presentation of history. However, the fact that a major portion of social studies teachers in the junior high school have a stronger background in history than in geography has brought the criticism that geography has been neglected since it was brought into the history courses.

Another criticism of social studies in today's schools is the stress on Western culture and the exclusion of Eastern culture. Much has been written in professional literature concerning the lack of study of Eastern culture in our schools but there has been very little move away from the Western-oriented program. Courses of study and textbooks for the junior high school are beginning to include some phases of Eastern culture, in token recognition of the many criticisms in this direction.

One definite trend in social studies has been in the area of current events. This move resulted in a broadening of the social studies concept, but too often current events are taught in isolation from the course itself. Usually, one day a week is devoted to current events and the other four days are spent strictly within the confines of the textbook.

The social studies concept of a broad coverage of the many related subjects is not a new one but it has not been fully realized. The Report of the Committee of Ten of the National Education Association, published in 1893, used the term *social studies*, but the concept of the Committee was rather narrow and referred largely to the areas of history and government. It seems strange that the broader concept has not been used nearly so well in social studies as in other curricular areas. The broad "general" science concept is widely accepted in the junior high school, as is the broader idea of the language arts. The modern trend in mathematics is toward general courses that break across the traditional lines between arithmetic, algebra, geometry, and so on. These subject areas seem to fit well into the exploratory and transition functions of the junior high school. In the area of social studies, however, very little has been done to develop a sequence of courses that would give the adolescent child an opportunity to explore the various facets of this all-important area of human relationships. It would seem that such a move is in keeping with the pattern of the other subject matter areas of the junior high school and with the functions of the school.

Science.   Although the impact of Sputnik and the National Defense Education Act have had an influence on the growth of the junior high school science program, it would be unfair to attribute our present programs to these two factors. Science at the ninth-grade level has been with us for a rather long period. Science instruction in Grades 7 and 8, however, has been growing at a rapid rate since World War II.

"General" science was introduced into the ninth grade as more or less a survey course. This program has traditionally carried elements of biological, physical, and earth sciences. The functions of these courses were:

1. To provide a background for those who would go into the specialized science in senior high school;
2. To provide exploratory experiences so that pupils could better face the problem of electing science courses at the senior high school level;
3. To provide an opportunity for all pupils to gain an insight into science even though they would not take other science courses later in the senior high school.

Following the establishment of the ninth-grade course, the subject was gradually pushed downward into Grades 7 and 8. In most cases, the program was on a half-year basis in these grades or on a basis of two or three periods per week. The pattern today in Grades 7 and 8 varies to a wide degree. Some schools offer full-time courses at all grade levels while others offer it only in one grade or alternate it with other subjects on a part-time basis.

The science program in the unreorganized junior high school has caused considerable duplication of effort. Very often the content of the courses in Grades 7 and 8 duplicates the programs offered in Grade 9. This causes many problems when several different eight-year elementary schools send their students to the same four-year high school. Some pupils will have had a part-time science program and others will have had two full years of formal science instruction. In such a situation the instructor at the ninth-grade level finds himself with a class composed of pupils with varying backgrounds. He finds it difficult to teach any material that has not been covered to at least some degree by at least a portion of his class.

The science textbook, which is common to most classrooms, usually serves as the course of study for the three-year sequence in junior high school. Research concerned with the use, reliability, and effectiveness of the textbook and workbook in science is rather meager. Perhaps this can be accounted for by the widespread condemnation of the "textbook" method among science educators. Although this condemnation may have encouraged research in the field, it has had very little effect on the teachers who do the actual instruction.

The presence of textbooks and the lack of other resource science materials at this grade level have forced teachers into the textbook method. However, with a national emphasis on science education, more and more resource materials are being developed and made available. As time goes on, we will find more courses of study that are not tied to the single textbook.

The laboratory method of teaching has never really flourished at the junior high school level. Demonstrations by the teacher have been the traditional pattern with the actual use of laboratory equipment by the pupil being delayed until senior high school. Funds from the National Defense Education Act have helped to correct this, as money is now available to provide materials, equipment, and space to make laboratory experiences a reality in the junior high school.

In recent years, some schools have been moving biology downward from Grade 10 to Grade 9, thus pushing the ninth-grade general science down into Grades 7 and 8. However, the more common pattern seems to be the development of a strong three-year sequence of general science courses in the junior high school which meets the general education needs for certain pupils, yet provides an excellent background for those going on into senior high school courses. Although the sequence of courses is still dominated by a textbook series, many schools are moving toward a sequence that would place earth and biological sciences in Grades 7 and 8 with a strong course in physical science completing the sequence at the ninth-grade level. The Science Manpower Project[9] has suggested the following broad units for the junior high school sequence:

Grade 7: "The Environment and Human Needs"
1. The Earth in Space
2. The Atmosphere
3. Water Resources
4. Biological Resources[10]

Grade 8: "The Use and Control of Energy"
1. Structure of Matter
2. Transformation of Energy
3. Man and Machines
4. The Body and How it Works[11]

Grade 9: "Frontiers of Science"
1. Our Atomic World
2. Planet Earth
3. Maintenance of Health
4. Science and Change[12]

The above recommendation, like many others, are not intended to be rigid for all schools, but merely point out the idea that each school system needs a clearly defined sequence of science experiences through the junior high school years. A national pattern of this sort would be valuable in dealing with the transfer problems created by our highly mobile population. However, individual schools can do very little in this area. The major emphasis of each school system must therefore be in the direction of developing a sequence of science experiences, not just for the junior high school, but for the entire local program from kindergarten through the twelfth grade.

Foreign languages. Modern foreign languages are relatively new to the public junior high school. The ninth grade has offered courses for years in the four-year senior high school and this was

---

[9] Abraham S. Fischler, *Modern Junior High School* (New York: Teachers College, Columbia University, 1961).
[10] *Ibid.*, pp. 9–24.
[11] *Ibid.*, pp. 45–76.
[12] *Ibid.*, pp. 77–107.

incorporated into the ninth grade of the reorganized junior high school. Only in recent years, however, has the movement toward a full sequence in the total junior school taken form.

At one time there was an effort in the direction of "general languages" which followed the "general science" concept. An example of this was a program described by McWilliams[13] for gifted junior high school students. The "World Languages" program provided an orientation in five languages and cultures.

The "general languages" program was never widespread and the direction has generally been toward a single language studied over a period of several years. This type of program was based on a "cultural" rather than a "linguistic" approach to the study of a foreign language. Since World War II, there has been a decided trend away from an emphasis on culture in the study of a language and toward an emphasis on the mastery of linguistic skills. In the same manner, emphasis is more and more on the speaking skills rather than on the reading skills.

The trend toward the audio-linguistic approach is tied directly to the feeling of a need for better world understanding through direct communication. This general feeling among our national leaders has been a major factor in pushing the foreign language program of the senior high school into the junior high school.

With foreign languages still not established in the junior high school, foreign language instruction in the elementary school was encouraged. In January, 1953, Dr. Earl J. McGrath, then U.S. Commissioner of Education, organized a conference on the Role of Foreign Languages in American Schools and the part to be played by the elementary school was emphasized. The fact that the recommendations of this conference received national attention influenced foreign language instruction in the junior high school. Although the junior high school was not largely considered in the publicity, there was considerable interest developed for the introduction of language programs at this level.

One of the major factors working against foreign languages in the junior high school is the shortage of qualified teachers. The audio-lingual approach requires instructional competencies that

---

13 Earl M. McWilliams, "Enrichment Practices for Gifted Junior High School Pupils," *Bulletin of National Association of Secondary School Principals,* Vol. 40, No. 221 (September, 1956), 73.

many teachers do not have at the present time. Conant's[14] recommendations for bilingual teachers is evidence of this demand but teachers are not yet available in sufficient numbers to fill the demands.

The introduction of foreign languages into the curriculum is causing another problem in the junior high school. Traditionally, the program of studies at the seventh- and eighth-grade levels has been one of common learning and most courses have been required of all students. Languages present a problem in that while they are "skills" courses there are serious questions as to whether or not they should be required of all students or provided only for the superior student. It also poses the question of what existing courses in an already full program the foreign language is to replace. If the course is to be an elective, it immediately goes into competition with practical arts such as home economics and industrial arts. Such a situation places the language in a poor position as the active junior high school student will usually be more attracted to the exercise of physical skills in the industrial arts shop or in the home economics laboratory.

At present, the trend seems to be toward providing languages for the better student on a "selective" basis rather than an "elective" basis. The more able student is "selected" and "guided" into the foreign language program while the less able student is placed in programs of reading improvement. Thus, foreign languages are not placed in a competitive position where they would not be likely to meet with success.

There is definitely a move toward more and more foreign languages in the junior high school but they are not yet an established part of the program. Again, as in other subject matter areas, such a program of foreign languages must be a planned sequence of experiences. If the linguistic values are to be realized, the program of the junior high school must be in step with the program of the senior high school. Only under such an arrangement can sufficient time be devoted to developing usable linguistic skills. An isolated junior high school program in languages can be justified if it is to emphasize the culture, but it cannot be justified on a basis of a linguistic emphasis.

---

[14] James B. Conant, *The Junior High School Years* (Princeton, N.J.: Educational Testing Service, 1960), p. 18.

The time element in an already overcrowded program of studies is another of the major difficulties encountered by those who wish to introduce foreign languages. Van Til, Vars, and Lounsbury[15] cite examples of schools using shorter periods of time for introductory foreign languages in Grades 7 and 8 with a full course on an elective basis at Grade 9.

The fine arts and practical arts. The crowded time schedule in most junior high schools has led to the offering of many subjects on a part-time basis. The fine arts and practical arts very often fall into this category and are commonly offered on a so-called exploratory basis. The major objective of such programs is to provide opportunities for junior high pupils to have a wide range of experiences in the various fields, not to insist on the development of specialized skills. The organization of these exploratory programs varies from school to school both in time allotments and in course offerings. The more common course offerings in the fine arts are music, dramatics, and visual arts. The practical arts may include industrial arts, home economics, and typewriting. Few schools offer all these courses for all pupils. The usual pattern is to select some of the courses for all pupils and make certain other courses electives.

Some of the administrative patterns of organization that have been used with success are shown in the following charts.

The Quarter-Year plan (see Fig. 3–1) would make it possible to offer exploration in five subject areas yet would use only one period

9 Weeks	9 Weeks	9 Weeks	9 Weeks
Music	Art	Typewriting	Home Economics (*girls*)
			Industrial Arts (*boys*)

Fig. 3–1. Quarter-Year Courses.

of a pupil's school day. More courses could be introduced in a shorter period of time with the variation shown in Fig. 3–2.

1st Semester		2nd Semester		
9 Weeks	9 Weeks	6 Weeks	6 Weeks	6 Weeks
Typewriting	Music	Drama	Art	Home Economics (*girls*)
				Industrial Arts (*boys*)

Fig. 3–2. Short-Course Schedule.

[15] Van Til, Vars and Lounsbury, *Modern Education for the Junior High School Years* (New York: The Bobbs-Merrill Company, 1961), pp. 371–72.

The six-week programs in drama, art, home economics, and industrial arts are rather short, but if they are repeated over the three years of junior high school, then the time allotment appears to be better. It must also be remembered that these programs are exploratory in nature and highly developed skills are not necessarily expected.

The Semester Plan (see Fig. 3–3) could provide these experiences over a longer period of time but certain courses would have to be deleted or additional time would have to be found for them. This plan would permit a teacher to offer a course for a full semester during one year instead of breaking it into nine week periods for two years.

Grade	1st Semester	2nd Semester
7	Drama	Art
8	Industrial Arts (*boys*) Home Economics (*girls*)	Typewriting
9	Electives for Two Semesters	
	Art Typewriting Home Economics	Industrial Arts Drama

Fig. 3–3. Semester Plan Schedule.

Some of the areas in the arts can be taught in short class periods while others require full-length periods. For example, industrial arts and home economics require at least full periods because of the need to set up equipment and to clean up at the end of each period. A twenty-five- or thirty-minute home economics period would place serious limitations on the experiences that could be offered. On the other hand, a shorter period in typewriting, drama, or music could possibly be effectively used. Consideration of this element has resulted in a combination-type schedule of exploration (see Fig. 3–4).

1st Semester	2nd Semester
9 Weeks	*9 Weeks*
Drama (25 minutes) Art	Home Economics (*girls:* 50 minutes)
Typewriting (25 minutes)	Industrial Arts (*boys:* 50 minutes)

Fig. 3–4. Combination Schedule.

Any junior high school can offer an exploratory program in the arts if the desire to do so is present. How elaborate the program is to be and how much time is to be devoted to it depends upon the facilities available. The wide range of possibilities in such a program reduces the schedule problems. It is difficult for a school to justify the lack of these areas in the instructional program if the exploratory, guidance, and transitional functions of the junior high school are to be recognized and fulfilled.

Visual arts.   Although the various specialized areas of design, drawing, painting, ceramics, weaving, and the like may be offered in the junior high school, it appears that a generalized art program is more adapted to the functions of the school. It would seem wiser to introduce the pupils to the many media of expression offered by the arts over this three-year period.

It can be assumed that children have had some art experiences by the time they reach the junior high school. The function, in Grades 7, 8, and 9, must be to help them gain more advanced skills and techniques with familiar materials and also to learn to work creatively with new ones. Some of the more commonly stated objectives are:

1. To develop an interest in art expression;
2. To understand vocational opportunities in art;
3. To appreciate good design and workmanship;
4. To develop an appreciation for contemporary art forms;
5. To learn something of major artists;
6. To develop skills for recreational use;
7. To become familiar with various art processes and materials;
8. To learn some specific holiday and seasonal applications of art.

Industrial arts.   The working media of industrial arts in the junior high school are too often only wood and metal. However, plastics, stone, plaster, and other materials are found in some programs. Frequently, the overlapping "crafts" areas could be considered part of either the arts or industrial arts areas, and this has prompted some schools to move in the direction of a unified arts and industries program. In this type of program the pupil has the opportunity to work in any media necessary to complete his experience. The combination art room and shop facility offers much flexibility and a more closely integrated experience.

The objectives of the industrial arts program in Grades 7, 8, and 9 are best achieved through the general shop program rather than through specialized offerings. The program should be organized along general education lines if it is to meet the needs of this age group. This is not to say that all vocational aspects of the program should be ignored, for the guidance function must be realized in any exploration program. Some of the major objectives of industrial arts in the junior high school are:

1. To develop an understanding of industry and the methods of production;
2. To provide satisfying experiences in self-expression;
3. To provide opportunities for self-discovery of interests and aptitudes, leading toward maturing life interests;
4. To develop appreciations for good design and good workmanship, and thus judgment and resourcefulness in selection, purchase and care of products;
5. To develop ability to use tools and materials for household maintenance, leisure-time pursuits, and—in some degree—basic occupational skills;
6. To develop ability to read and make drawings used for illustrative and constructive purposes;
7. To develop safety habits and safety consciousness not only in the school but also in the home.

The wide range of tools and materials available make it impossible for a pupil to become proficient in all. But, the competent instructor can give a wide range of valuable experiences to pupils of varying abilities and interests.

Industrial arts offerings in the junior high school need not be confined to boys. The objectives of such a program can contribute much to the general education of girls as well.

Home economics.   Although home economics may be offered to both boys and girls in the junior high schools, it is usually offered in separate classes. At this level, girls are usually more mature than boys and their interests and needs are somewhat different. The objectives for a home economics program for either boys or girls may be stated in general terms, but the emphasis and activities must be adapted to the group to be served. Some of the commonly stated objectives are:

1. To learn to work and share in group activities;
2. To develop an understanding and an appreciation for the activities and responsibilities of the homemaker;
3. To develop skills in the selection, use, and care of equipment, furnishing, clothing, and food;
4. To plan, prepare, and serve food and simple meals;
5. To understand the relationship between adequate diet and health;
6. To develop the basic understanding of the uses of color in food, clothing, and home decorations;
7. To develop an understanding in the care of children and the responsibilities of babysitting;
8. To develop certain basic skills in the preparation of foods, the construction and care of clothing, and home decoration;
9. To develop interests and skills in worthy leisure-time activities in the home.

Activities in such a program are varied and may range from food preparation and clothing construction to activities involved in babysitting. Personal grooming activities are usually stressed as well as personal budgeting of money.

Music. Although music is sometimes offered as a part of the exploratory sequence, more often it is scheduled to alternate with physical education or some other part-time course. In some schools it is scheduled separately, with "general" and vocal music as required courses and instrumental instruction provided on an elective or selective basis.

The general music concept is very much in keeping with the exploratory function of the junior high school. It provides an opportunity for all pupils to become familiar with music. However, the general music program is not sufficient to meet the needs of all junior high school pupils. General music can be taught on a group basis and include children with varying backgrounds of music experiences. On the other hand, there is a distinct need to go beyond this basic concept and provide some specialized experiences for those who have interest and ability in this area. The work beyond the general music program requires more organization and variation in presentation. Many junior high school pupils have had specialized music training at the elementary level and others have a desire to start concentrated work on music. Such a situation requires a certain amount of grouping and individualized instruction if the objectives are to be realized. Some schools provide individualized instruction during the school day while others require that time outside the school day be used. In many cases, a pupil who wishes to become a part of the school instrumental group may have to take lessons privately as sufficient school personnel is not available to offer individual instruction. In the final analysis, a junior high school instrumental program depends on several factors: whether the elementary music program produces pupils able to work with a group; whether the economic and cultural level of the community will provide private instruction; and whether there are available in the school music teachers who can provide individual instruction for the beginner. A combination of these factors will determine how far a school can go in providing music instruction for all pupils. The general music program can reach all pupils but specialized instruction can be extended only as far as the circumstances within the school and community permit.

Creative drama.   In junior high school, the word *creative* should be the key for this phase of exploration. Too many of our classes emphasize the copying of lessons, the following of directions, and the memorizing of facts. It is in this neglected area—creativity —that drama can make its most valuable contribution.

Pupils need not necessarily produce plays written by established authors. Instead it seems more logical, under the creative concept, that the pupils take human problems, emotions, triumphs, and activities for presentation in living drama. This would require them to give their own interpretation and expression to a given situation.

Activities in such a program of instruction could well start with simple action pantomimes such as tying shoes, wrapping a gift package, or hitting a baseball. This sort of activity could be followed by mood pantomime which would be expressive of activities that result in surprise, pleasure, or anger.

The next step is that of adding speech to the mood pantomime. Here again, the emphasis should be on self-expression with the pupil speaking spontaneously rather than reading from a written script. With the introduction of dialogue, the class may then progress to dramatizing parts of familiar stories or events. This could lead to the dramatization of original or familiar literature in which the pupils give their own expression to the characters involved.

Objectives of this type of program may be expressed as follows:

1. To encourage initiative on the part of the pupil in expression and criticism of dramatization;
2. To help the pupil achieve controlled and balanced emotions;
3. To provide opportunities for cooperative action in the group situation;
4. To foster sound attitudes and to gain effective control over the body;
5. To help the pupil express himself fluently and with flexibility;
6. To help the pupil gain a deep and sympathetic understanding of his fellow man;
7. To develop an active and creative imagination.

Typewriting. Typewriting is basically a skills course and the stress on these skills is an inherent part of the instruction. However, the exploratory function of such instruction cannot place the high premium on skills that would be found in the vocational program in the senior high school. Through instruction, the pupil should gain an understanding of the value of the typewriter as a device for communication and develop some personal skills in its use.

The seventh-grade instructor should endeavor to develop a knowledge of the typewriter keyboard and the various operative parts of the machine. Attention should also be given to building manipulative skills so that the seventh-grader can approach the typewriter with ease and comfort. The eighth and ninth grades would refine the basic skills and understandings as well as going further in the personal uses of the machine.

After some degree of proficiency has been developed, opportunities should be given for pupils to make practical use of the typewriter. At least one period each week should be provided for using the machine in preparing lessons for other classes and for personal uses. In addition, typewriters should be made available during study periods or after school hours so that the pupil may use his newly acquired skills in other phases of his school and personal life.

Health and physical education. The nature of the student body of the junior high school makes the problem of health and physical education complex. The wide range of physical and emotional maturity during these years places the physical education program in a position not found in the elementary school nor in the senior high school. The wide variation in maturity demands a physical education program that will meet the needs and interests of the pre-adolescent, the early adolescent, and the late adolescent. It should be obvious that such a demand cannot be met by a narrow range of activities. At this level the physical education must cover a wide range of activities and these must be adjusted to the various levels of physical maturity found in the junior high school.

The heart of the health and physical education program, like that of other subject areas, must be in the organized class activities. Providing for voluntary participation in intramural and interscholastic sports and making facilities available for recreational activities are all a part of a physical education program but these activities should be offered in addition to the organized classwork. By the same token, "incidental" teaching of health is no substitute for a regularly organized instructional program in health education. The health services of the school and incidental teaching of health are essential parts of the health program, but cannot replace organized health instruction.

Classes in physical education should maintain a proper balance of body-building exercises, individual and team games, testing activities, and provisions for remedial and corrective measures. Emphasis must be on physical skills that have value in out-of-school activities and in later adult life. Care must be taken that seasonal sports do not cause an imbalance in the program. Too often the needs and real interests of the majority are limited by the few who wish to concentrate on the team sport that is in season.

Care must also be taken to consider the physical maturity of the junior high school pupil. Some are capable of strenuous exercise and can develop the skills of the senior high school student, but the majority are not ready for this sort of program. It is perhaps wiser to place the more highly competitive activities outside the framework of class instruction and offer them to those with ability and interest in a well-rounded intramural program. Such a plan offers the activities for those who can profit from them but does not force all pupils into such a pattern.

Health education is commonly shared with the class time of other subjects. Very often it is taught in connection with science or as a part of the "core" or "block of time" program. Some schools regularly alternate two periods of health education with three periods of physical education.

There seems to be a recent trend toward testing in physical education. Standards for physical achievements are being developed and testing is now being conducted on a rather wide scale. It must be recognized that this movement is not an end in itself. As in other areas, it is only a starting point. Testing can serve a definite need if it is used to identify problems and then proper steps are taken to diagnose and correct deficiencies. Testing alone, however, wastes money and wastes the time of both teachers and pupils.

Summary

The generalized courses seem to be in keeping with the functions of the junior high school. These are most adaptable to providing guidance and exploratory experiences and at the same time offer many opportunities for the transition from the emphasis on basic learning skills of the elementary school to the more specialized subject matter-oriented program of the senior high school.

Since the inception of the junior high school, there have always been those forces that have pushed in the direction of a little senior high school. Unfortunately these efforts have been too successful and often the real justification for the junior high school has been lost. The transition from the elementary school to the senior high school cannot be adequately accomplished with an early senior high school program. Too often the work on the basic skills is terminated at the end of Grade 6 and the subject matter specialist takes over with the assumption that the seventh-grader has mastered the basic skills and is completely ready for subject matter specialization.

The current trend seems to be toward pushing more and more of the subject matter materials of the senior high school downward to the junior high school. Such a movement does have some merit if handled in an intelligent manner, but it is not an easy task. Too often geometry is moved to Grade 9 and algebra to Grades 7 and 8. It is true that certain geometric and algebraic concepts can be taught at lower grade levels. However, the practice of moving a complete course from the senior high school to the junior high school can meet with disastrous results.

The junior high school is in a position to operate a very flexible program as it is removed from the domination of the college. This flexibility in the scheduling of time and broad course content must be maintained or the advantages of the school will be lost. The "block of time" or "core" courses represent one phase of flexibility.

Teachers and administrators should recognize the unique functions and strength of the junior high school program and curriculum planning should be carried on within the structure of those functions. If these functions are not observed in the planning, the effectiveness of the program will be seriously impaired and the junior high school will cease to make a definite contribution to the transitional period of our youth.

CHAPTER IV

The Extraclass Program

The very nature of the instructional program of the junior high school necessitates a wide range of out-of-class activities if the individual needs of the pupil are to be met. The major administrative device of the senior high school in providing for individual differences is the program of elective courses. Under this organization the pupil has an opportunity to select courses that are most challenging to his interest and abilities. A broad range of elective courses is missing in most junior high schools, and the emphasis on the common learnings places serious restrictions on the possibilities of meeting specialized needs and interests of the pupils. This lack of possibilities for elective experiences in the program must be compensated for in the over-all curriculum offerings and the most efficient way of doing this is through the extraclass phases of the curriculum. There is a high degree of justification for the emphasis on common learnings in the classroom organization, but to complete the functions of transition, exploration, and guidance, these learnings must be supplemented with activities outside the classroom structure.

Although a wide range of extraclass activities can be justified in any school, the major portion must supplement the classroom work. For this reason those activities that are an outgrowth of the classroom program are most easily justified. For example, the science club is an opportunity for the interested pupil with ability to go far beyond classroom work. In the same way, intramural sports permit the boy or girl with interest and superior ability to go far beyond the general physical education program. In a similar manner, the drama club supplements the language arts classroom activities in speech and the special music groups offer experiences for those willing to devote extra time to them.

There are many extraclass activities that are not directly connected with the classroom program but can be justified as a part of the total curriculum. However, this type of activity should be carefully selected and scrutinized before it becomes part of the curriculum. The interested science teacher will devote the necessary time to his science club as will the music teacher to his small groups. But, many of the clubs and activities not connected with the subject matter areas are often poorly organized and badly managed because of the lack of background and interest of the teacher assigned to them.

Another consideration should be the community feeling toward the extraclass program. It is very easy to "sell" the idea of a science club as a part of the total science program, but a hiking club may be questioned if it interferes with the instructional program and cannot be connected in some way with the curriculum of the physical education department. Taxpayers are primarily interested in a program with a major emphasis on classroom instruction. They are very likely to criticize activities that are not directly tied to this program as being entertainment that should be sponsored by other organizations.

Another area of activity that should be studied carefully is that offered by other organizations in the community. The extraclass program is already too heavy in most junior high schools for it to take in activities that are being satisfactorily offered by other agencies. The school should not enter into competition with other agencies in the community but should cooperate with the community in offering opportunities to the young people that are not being met in other ways. Too often, camping and out-of-door education programs have failed when the school has attempted to duplicate the Boy Scout or Girl Scout programs. If the out-of-door education program is to be successful, it must make definite contributions to the existing school curriculum of science, mathematics, art, and other areas.

Certain activities of the service type, such as the safety patrol, the audio-visual club, and the library club, can be justified on a sound basis even though they are not a direct outgrowth of a classroom instructional program. Such activities not only offer a service to the total school program but also provide some very valuable experiences and meet certain needs of pupils that are not provided for in other phases of the curricular offerings.

Administration of the Extraclass Program

Like any other phase of the curriculum, the extraclass program must be well-organized and properly administered if it is to succeed.

Here are some of the recommended principles to follow in the organization and administration of the program:

1. *Qualified and interested teachers should be assigned to sponsorship.* As in any other phase of the curriculum the teacher is one of the major factors in the extraclass program. An administrator would not consider assigning to a mathematics class a teacher who has had no training in mathematics and who has no interest in the subject. This same principle should apply to extraclass assignments if the activities are to be worthwhile and make a curricular contribution.

2. *Sponsorship of an activity should be considered in the total work load of the teacher.* The practice of providing extra pay for sponsoring activities is questionable and should be studied carefully before being adopted as a policy. A busy teacher has time limitations and extra pay will not solve the problem of providing time to organize and operate a club program properly. Extra time rather than extra pay is needed. If an activity makes a worthwhile contribution to the instructional program, it must be considered in planning the work load of the teacher involved.

3. *Adequate time and a conflict-free schedule must be provided.* Many authorities advocate that all extraclass activities be allotted time during the school day. This is desirable as far as it is practical, but it must be recognized that the school day, crowded with required curriculum work, cannot be further crowded by adding a wide range of extraclass activities. Some activities can and should be scheduled during the school day but many must be scheduled outside the regular school hours. A few years ago, the 8 A.M.–4 P.M. school day was shortened. The extra free hours, in many cases, are used for questionable leisure-time activities and there is little reason to limit the use of these after-school hours to elective school activities.

Children of junior high school age are interested in a wide range of activities and should be permitted to explore as many of these as is feasible. There is a limit to the time available to do all the things they wish but an effort should be made to schedule extraclass activities so that there will be as few conflicts as possible. The classroom schedule is very carefully organized to reduce conflicts in scheduling. The same care should be taken in scheduling the extraclass program.

4. *Eligibility for participation should be very flexible.* Too often, eligibility requirements for participation in an activity defeat the purpose of the activity. Scholastic achievement is one of the most commonly used devices for determining eligibility and very often this measure disqualifies the pupils who could profit most from the activity. Success in a major portion of classroom activity is usually most easily attained by the child with verbal ability. The school

should provide opportunities for the nonverbal child to be successful in nonverbal activities. If scholastic success is used as the criterion for participation in the extraclass program, many pupils will be eliminated from the few experiences from which they can profit most.

The socio-economic levels of our society play a very important role in participation in activities. It is usually difficult to get participation from the lower socio-economic levels. If fees are charged and the organizations are socially selective, then those children who could profit most are often eliminated.

5. *A major portion of the extraclass activities should be a direct outgrowth of the classroom instructional program.* One of the major contributions of the extraclass program is the provision of opportunities for the child who can go far beyond the work that is offered in the conventional classroom. The school that provides fully for individual differences in the classroom can justify a smaller extraclass program.

Service activities.   The service clubs of the school not only provide opportunities for many pupils to have rich experiences but also add much to the total school program. Whenever possible, such activities should be connected with an instructional area—but this is not always possible or desirable. The student council is an example of this sort of activity. It should be identified with social studies and sponsored by social studies teachers. Because of its nature, it cuts across several subject matter lines, but the basic principles of democratic government are a definite part of the social studies curriculum.

The audio-visual club and the library club are two other activities that are deeply involved in the total instructional program but cannot be identified with a specific subject matter area. As in the case of the Student Council, these provide services to the total school and offer many valuable experiences. The Future Nurses Club is a service rather than an instructional phase of the school. Actually, such a club could be considered as an outgrowth of health instruction, but in actual practice the health services are usually separate from health instruction.

Activities supplementing classroom instruction.   The vast majority of extraclass activities fall under this classification. School publications go far beyond the classroom activities of the language arts programs. The school newspaper and annual magazine offer a service to the school, but—more important—they offer a more specialized experience for those boys and girls with ability and interest in the journalistic phases of the language arts program. In some schools band, orchestra, and chorus activities are offered on an extraclass basis to provide opportunities beyond the general music program. However, the more common practice is to provide classroom time for these activities and to offer small-group instrumental and vocal ensembles on an extraclass basis.

The intramural program is a fully accepted extraclass phase of physical education, but there are many questions on the advisability of offering interscholastic athletics as an elective activity in the junior high school. Many persons seriously question whether junior high school pupils are either emotionally or physically mature enough to profit from the highly competitive and physically strenuous activities of interscholastic athletics. The intramural program offers the opportunities for participation in a mildly competitive situation and more nearly fits the transitional and exploratory functions of the junior high school program.

Guidance activities. One of the most widely used guidance activities of the junior high school is the homeroom. The organization of this activity is usually looked upon as a way of giving a more individualized guidance in the departmentalized organization of the secondary school. The change from the single teacher of the self-contained elementary school classroom to the many teachers of the departmentalized junior high school presents some serious problems in transition. The assignment of a pupil to a homeroom teacher fills a definite need in transition and guidance when this change occurs. It is most unfortunate that the homeroom is too often used as an administrative device rather than as a guidance device. The schedule that provides ten to fifteen minutes daily for the homeroom has predesigned the activities and restricted them to administrative functions: keeping attendance records, collecting fees, and making announcements. Time is not available for guidance activities and, as a result, very little can be accomplished in this area. If the guidance function is to be realized in the homeroom, administrative details must be taken care of in other ways and longer periods must be provided on a one- or two-day-per-week basis. A regular sequence of experiences should be organized for all three grades for orientation to the junior high school, with experiences for orientation to senior high school planned for Grade 9. Units such as parliamentary procedure should be given in Grade 7 with units on boy-girl relationships and vocations in Grades 8 and 9. It would seem that the plans of the Commission on Staff Utilization of the National Association of Secondary School Principals[1] could be applied to this organization. The "large-group" plans and "small-group" plans will fit very well into such a situation. Several of the small homerooms could be brought together to see films and hear presentations prepared by outstanding teachers. The discussions, in turn, could be conducted in small-group situations under the various homeroom teachers. Such a plan would involve team teaching in which the teacher with the best background in the particular area under discussion would organize, prepare, and present the materials.

Other guidance activities commonly offered are in the areas of vocational interests. This would include such clubs as Future Farmers of America and Future Teachers Clubs. However, this type of activity is not so commonly found in the junior high school as it is in the senior high school. Junior high school activities are normally of the exploratory and general type. Specialized organizations have more success in the senior high school.

Recreational and social activities.   There is definitely a place in the junior high school for recreational and social activities. Although they are not directly tied to the classroom programs, they do provide opportunities for the development of certain skills and attitudes that are not taught in other phases of the curriculum. A dancing club may be justified for teaching the basic skills and courtesies, but a continuation of membership in such a club through the three years of junior high school is questionable. School dances should provide actual situations to use the skill rather than be used as extensions of formalized instruction. If such an instructional program can be provided in the physical education classes, it would serve the purpose, and a club of this sort would not then be necessary.

Assembly programs are usually in the category of recreational activities. Although most assembly programs do have instructional value, the recreational aspects of the program are probably their major contribution. Unless the instructional aspect of such programs is presented in an entertaining manner, its success is limited. Strictly instructional programs can probably be made more meaningful if

---

[1] J. Lloyd Trump and Dorsey Baynham, *A Guide to Better Schools* (Skokie, Ill.: Rand McNally & Co., 1961).

presented in the classroom where a follow-up can be provided with questions and an opportunity for discussion. Too often the value of an hour-long lecture in a large group is lost if it cannot be followed up with study and discussion in a smaller group.

Summary

The extraclass program of the junior high school should definitely be considered as part of the total instructional program. On the whole, it must be recognized that the main emphasis in instruction normally comes from the classroom—the primary instructional organization of the school. This is not to say that the extraclass program is of little value, but we must recognize that it is a supplementary device to strengthen the school program. Some aspects of instruction can be presented in a much more efficient manner in the extraclass program, but the major learnings of the school take place in the classroom.

The school that places too much emphasis on activities that cannot be justified from an instructional viewpoint is very likely to meet with opposition from the parents and the community. On the other hand, the school that does little work in extraclass activities is seriously curtailing its curricular offerings. The school that selects its extraclass offerings carefully and provides time and planning for the program will achieve good results and will find support in the community as a whole.

CHAPTER V

School Services

The heart of the school is its instructional program and any service of the school must be justified in terms of its contribution toward improving instruction. This is not to say that the service must be involved in instruction but that through its operation more effective instruction must be realized. Some services, such as remedial reading and speech correction, are primarily instructional in nature. Others, such as audio-visual and library services, contribute to instruction through materials and equipment. Guidance and health services make their contributions in promoting the well-being of the pupils while the maintenance and custodial services contribute by providing a climate within which the instructional program can operate in a more effective manner.

The Principal's Office

The first line of service in the instructional program should be the administrative offices. In many schools the principal's office is a combination business office, registrar's office, supply center, and clerical pool—besides furnishing the other services provided by the administration. The effectiveness of the services are determined, to a large degree, by the attitude of the administration toward the function of the office as a service agency. Many of the routine, time-consuming tasks of the teacher can—and should—be handled by clerical personnel in the administrative offices. Maintaining attendance records, collecting fees, typing, and duplicating materials consume much of the teachers' time and could be done just as effectively by nonprofessional, clerical personnel. The wise administrator will survey the services of his office from time to time and revise them when he can see ways to improve instruction through additional or different types of service.

In addition to the routine services that can be handled by clerical personnel, the administrator must also provide professional services.

In some schools, these will be handled by the principal; in larger schools, by additional professional personnel. Instruction may be supervised by the principal or delegated to other personnel provided by the administration. It should be pointed out that classroom visitation and supervision are not synonymous. Classroom visitation is but one facet of supervision. Instruction can be improved through supervisory techniques and devices that should be used by the effective administrator. In-service training programs, promotion of experimentation, curricular planning and development, personal conferences with teachers, and research are but a few of the devices that can be effectively used.

The maintenance and effective use of records can contribute much to the instructional program of a school. Herein lies a rich source of information that should be screened and tabulated in a continuing effort to find weak and strong aspects of the school and to find solutions to problems that arise from time to time.

The competent principal will strive to exert his professional leadership by making his office the primary service center of the school for both teachers and pupils. This may place a heavy work load on the offices but through efficient administration the office will become a busy and an effective service center.

The Library

The very nature of the junior high school program makes the library essential. It would be rather difficult to conceive of a program of transition that did not provide adequate facilities for the young student to explore his wide range of interests in a well-stocked library. An instructional program restricted to a textbook and a few volumes on the classroom shelf is likely to be very narrow in information and in points of view. An instructional program can be broad only if its resources are broad, and the primary resources of the school are books. If individual differences of pupils are to be met in the classroom, there must be a wide range of books to provide opportunities for their various levels of ability.

The dominant pattern of organization in the elementary school seems to be the classroom library while the senior high school most commonly has a centralized library. This places the junior high school in a situation of needing to provide adequate library services

that will introduce the independent use of reference materials before
pupils reach senior high school. In situations where the elementary
school does provide an adequate centralized library, the junior high
school must continue this facility if it is to capitalize on the study
skills developed in the elementary school.

It is important that the library of the junior high school be organized along the standard lines of other libraries so that library
skills will be developed that may be used in the future. It would seem
essential that the Dewey decimal system be used and that proper
instruction in its use be made a part of the program. However, the
instruction should be integrated with the actual use of the library
rather than taught in isolation from the subject matter areas in which
it is to be used.

Instruction in the use of the library is not the only instructional
function of the librarian. A more difficult and complex problem
arises in the in-service training of the teaching staff on how to make
effective use of the library in the instructional program. Instruction
of pupils in the use of the library is useless unless the classroom
teacher gives the type of assignments that require use of library
materials and also provides time for actual use of the library facilities. This requires extreme tact and ingenuity on the part of the
administration and the library staff if teachers are to be weaned
away from textbook teaching and introduced to the broader program that the library offers.

The effective librarian must work closely with the teacher in the
selection of books and in the selection of services for their utilization. The librarian cannot possibly know the intricate details of the
classroom program and the materials that will best contribute to
that program. Books ordered by the librarian alone will not be used
by the teacher to the extent that jointly selected books will be used.
Ideally, the procurement of books should be initiated by the teacher
but from a practical point of view this does not work. Balance in the
library inventory must be maintained and teachers must be urged by
the librarian to improve the collection of works in their areas.

A very effective method of getting library utilization is a faculty
study of homework. A skillfully handled study of this sort should
evolve to a point at which the major interest will be in the type of
out-of-class assignments rather than the quantity of work to be done
at home. Quality assignments will result in increased library utili-

zation. It should be recognized that a faculty study of this sort must originate with the administration, but the librarian also has a stake in it.

The junior high school that provides study hall periods should make the library easily accessible to pupils assigned to study halls. If the longer class period is used, with supervised study included, then class time must be provided for the pupil to use the library. It is a common practice in some schools for a teacher to check out library materials for a particular unit of instruction and place them on the classroom shelf. This plan has merit in certain situations but should not be used exclusively. Junior high school pupils need to have an opportunity to develop the skills of finding their own materials in the library.

The effective library must be operated by a professionally trained librarian and equipped with the tools of book selection and library evaluation. Adequate work space must be provided, along with sufficient space for shelving of books, storage, and reading stations. Clerical assistants, either adults or students, must be provided if the librarian is to do a professional job. The absence of any of these elements will place a serious handicap on the contribution of the library to the instructional program.

Audio-Visual

There seems to be widespread agreement that the audio-visual facilities should be physically close to the library. However, there is considerable disagreement as to whether the audio-visual services should or should not be considered part of the library for administrative purposes. One argument for combining the two is that both work with instructional materials and separate administrative organizations will tend to duplicate services or, in some cases, to omit some very important ones. Whether the library and audio-visual facilities are administered separately or together is unimportant as long as they serve the instructional program effectively. Administrative structures must be adapted to the unique needs and circumstances in particular schools.

Too often, the instructional value of an audio-visual program is evaluated on a quantitative basis—that is, the number of pieces of equipment available and the number of films or recordings used.

Although the quantitative aspects of the program are important, they do not automatically assure a quality program. Proper utilization of equipment and the introduction of newer equipment and materials are a vital part of the total services. The standard list of equipment—which includes motion picture projectors, slide projectors, film strip projectors, opaque projectors, phonographs, tape recorders, models, and charts—is now being supplemented with overhead projectors, television sets, and teaching machines. To commercially-prepared materials are being added teacher-prepared materials. This has placed the audio-visual services in a position of keeping the faculty informed in the uses of these new media and in the utilization and production of materials.

The concept of the library as merely a repository for books is outmoded. By the same token, the effective audio-visual center must be much more than a place to store and service equipment. In-service training is an essential part of the audio-visual services and provisions for a production center for instructional materials is very important. The access of pupils to the production center can do much to improve classroom instruction. Classroom recitations, often deadly repetitions of "what the book said," can be enlivened if the pupil has a place to produce charts, graphs, and pictures and to make recordings. In addition to producing materials, many pupils can profit by reviewing films and filmstrips presented in class or viewing materials not used in class. The same is true of tape recordings and phonograph records.

The audio-visual service can contribute much to the total instructional program if it is operated by a professional educator rather than by a combination mechanic-clerk.

The Guidance Services

If the junior high school is to fulfill its guidance function, it is essential that an organized guidance program be developed and staffed by adequately trained personnel. It is true that the guidance function of the junior high school should be met, to a large degree, by the instruction and activities of the curricular offerings. However, this phase of guidance must be coordinated and supplemented by an organized guidance service.

McLean,[1] in a study of practices in junior high schools, found a high degree of organization in the following aspects of guidance:

1. Student orientation.
2. Guidance records.
3. Counseling.
4. Testing.
5. In-service training of the staff. (In the study, however, it was evident that the organized program for in-service training of the staff was found less often than the other aspects of the program.)

Individual counseling is usually considered as one of the major functions of the guidance services. The counseling process differs from the advisement services and requires specialized personnel. It is time-consuming and can be effective only in the hands of a skillful person and with repeated sessions. Advisement, however, is the more common technique and is often handled by persons with less training and skill. Very often, the junior high school guidance program depends upon advisement, which is handled largely by the homeroom teacher. The homeroom teacher refers to guidance personnel pupils who are in need of counseling. Such a plan is a realistic approach in a situation where sufficient counseling service is not available.

Group guidance is another technique commonly used to reduce the load of the trained guidance staff. Much time can be saved by giving general background information to a larger group and then working with individuals. Such a procedure reduces the time that is often used by the counselor in presenting the general information he would normally give to each pupil individually. Group counseling, along the lines of the group therapy used by psychiatrists, offers some promise in this field, but its techniques are difficult to develop and too often these sessions degenerate into "gripe" sessions which are difficult to turn in a positive direction.

Testing programs usually take up a large portion of the time of the guidance personnel. The two types of tests most commonly found in the junior high school are intelligence tests and achievement tests. In addition to these, interest inventories and aptitude

---

[1] Paul E. McLean, "A Study of Guidance in Selected Texas Junior High Schools," *Bulletin, National Association of Secondary School Principals*, Vol. 46, No. 271 (February, 1962), 316–17.

tests are used to some degree and some schools use personality inventories, attitude scales, and other standardized devices.

Much time, energy, and effort is expended each year on the administration and scoring of tests, but the results are often used only in a very superficial manner. Too often, testing programs are evaluated on the basis of the number of tests administered rather than on the use made of the results to improve the instructional program. It must be recognized that one of the important functions of an organized guidance program is to make the results of the testing program meaningful and useful to the teaching personnel of the school. A testing program which consists of one achievement test with provisions for use of the results is much more effective than a wide range of tests the results of which are then hidden away in the files to collect dust. Too often schools attempt to improve their testing programs by adding more tests rather than by analyzing the results of the tests that are already in use.

In-service training of the staff is essential if a guidance program is to be successful. The departmentalized organization of the school promotes the feeling of the teacher that she is a subject matter specialist and has no responsibilities for problems that are not directly connected with the subject she teaches in the classroom. Effective guidance in the junior high school must depend upon full participation by the entire teaching staff and steps must be taken to involve the teachers in the program. Two commonly used methods of involving the teachers are definite advisory assignments at the homeroom level and the widespread use of case conferences in which teachers meet with the guidance director to discuss the problems of specific pupils. A systematic approach must be made to help the classroom teacher become more effective in such areas as interpreting tests, working with underachievers, and providing opportunities for the gifted.

Cumulative folders are considered a "must" in any organized guidance program. The self-contained classroom of the elementary school provides an excellent climate in which to fix responsibility for keeping this sort of record up-to-date. The departmentalized organization of the junior high school, however, requires a different plan if the records are to be kept up-to-date and used effectively. A central file of folders and information on all pupils must be maintained and made easily accessible to the instructional staff.

In addition to the individual folders, group records should be available. It is a time-consuming task for teachers to go through the individual folder of each child assigned to her several classes. To avoid this, the guidance services should provide group records in which test scores and other records can be found without going through hundreds of individual folders. It is true that the individual folder contains specific information that cannot easily be placed in a group record but there are many times that a teacher needs to make a rapid survey of her class, and group records can help save much time.

Orientation is another very important function of the guidance services. The individual teacher is limited in what she can accomplish in the way of a broad orientation into the various aspects of junior high school life. Individual teachers can contribute much to such a program if it is well-coordinated and organized so that there are minimum overlaps and gaps in the total program.

Although orientation should be an on-going and continuous part of the junior high school program, there should be an emphasis on it early in Grade 7 and late in Grade 9. Very often schools start their orientation to the junior high school with visits of guidance personnel to the elementary school. Sixth-graders' orientation to the junior high school has proven very successful as have orientation programs for their parents. It is also essential that stress be placed on orientation during the early part of the seventh grade. General information given before the pupil enters the junior high school becomes much more meaningful when he is involved in the specifics of the program. Care must be taken to see that the pupil understands the procedures of the new school as he progresses into its activities.

Prior to the time the ninth-grader moves into the senior high school, he should be given a picture of what he is to expect. New procedures, new teachers, and new courses will cause him much concern unless he has an idea of the situations he is likely to meet. Sensible selection of elective courses for the tenth grade could mean the difference between a high school graduate and a dropout.

Curriculum development is another very important phase of the work of guidance personnel. Very often the solution to many of the serious problems in the junior high school could be found in curriculum revisions. Guidance personnel are usually in a position to see these problems much more clearly than other personnel of the school. Curricular content and activities are indeed a concern of the guidance staff and any curriculum committee that is working on revision of the program must include a representative of the guidance staff.

Health Services

The health services of the school should be a part of the educative process but not necessarily a part of the structural program of the health education classes. Health services can and should supplement the classroom instruction in health but they have a different function to perform in the total educational program.

Health service, like guidance, is basically a personal and individual affair. The relationship between the school nurse or doctor and the pupil is personal and very often loses its meaning in a group situation. It is true that health instruction on a group basis can accomplish certain objectives—as can group counseling—but the one-to-one ratio of a nurse to a pupil in an eye or ear check is a situation in which meaningful instruction can be conducted on an individual basis.

Health services in the school should not attempt to duplicate or replace the medical care provided by the family physician. On the contrary, the school should provide only emergency and advisory services, referring pupils to the proper agencies for diagnosis and treatment. The school is in a position to notice early symptoms of deviations from the norm and to refer the parents to the proper place for correction. Such a process is educative for both the pupil and the parent.

The most common services rendered by the school are eye and ear checks and immunization programs. The latter are usually undertaken in cooperation with the local medical association. In all cases, the contacts between the health personnel and the pupil should be fully explained and the results of the tests made known to both parents and children. Only through this sort of procedure can the educational values of the program be realized.

Health records are an integral part of the services. These should be kept up-to-date and accurate. They should be designed to reflect changes. Records of height and weight are meaningless at any one time but are important over a period of time.

In addition to the records of routine school checks, a medical record should be in the file of each child. Health information concerning illnesses, surgery, abnormalities, and other medical details can be of value to the school. Recommendations from doctors on special provisions for the child should be on file and teachers informed about them.

Some schools offer health checks, which are made with the cooperation of local doctors. However, in communities where it is possible, the practice of requiring periodic examinations by the family doctor seems to be preferable. Such a procedure encourages the child and the family to establish a routine that should continue after the relationship with the formal school program is terminated. However, schools on this plan are obligated to make some arrangements for those pupils who cannot engage the services of a doctor because of economic reasons.

Clinical Services

Clinical services for remedial and corrective education in the junior high school are not new but their development has been rather slow. A very large junior high school may employ a full-time reading clinician or speech therapist, but the usual pattern is to share such specialists with other schools in a system. The mathematics clinician is another specialist found in some schools, but rarely in junior high schools.

The primary function of this sort of a specialist is usually thought of as remedial and corrective work. However, an emerging pattern is to use these specialists in a consultative role as well. The emphasis is often in a total reading or speech improvement program that attempts to improve the instructional program for all boys and girls instead of dealing only with the few who have serious difficulties.

Remedial reading services have long been used in the elementary school and it has become evident that such services are also desirable at the junior high school level. The need for consultative services in reading has multiplied with the more rigid departmentalization that demand subject matter specialization on the part of the teacher rather than training in the teaching of basic skills. If the junior high school is to continue its work in refining the basic skills of the elementary school and also develop a high degree of subject matter specialization, it becomes mandatory for an administrative framework to be developed to keep both functions in proper perspective. The remedial reading teacher and consultant is one answer to this problem.

The reading specialist who acts both as a clinician and as a consultant can provide valuable services to the total instructional program. In the remedial role, the specialist must conduct the usual survey testing to determine the cases which require attention and provide the corrective instruction necessary for the individuals concerned. On the other hand, in the consultative role, the specialist can determine the over-all needs of the school and work with the classroom teachers in a broad reading improvement program that will benefit all the children. In actual practice, there is a danger that the reading specialist will be loaded with so many individual remedial cases that little time may be left to devote to the total reading improvement program. If careful value judgments are made, certain of the remedial cases can be dropped in order to provide time for the improvement services.

The pattern of speech correction work in the school is similar to that of remedial reading. The clinician usually makes a "sweep check" of the total student body and from this selects those pupils who require individual programs of speech correction. It is true that every school will have a number of boys and girls in need of individual work. However, the speech therapist who can reduce the individual cases and devote more time to working with the classroom teacher can contribute much more to the total program of the school.

One method of reducing the time required for remedial instruction is to organize pupils into groups. Group remedial work in reading, mathematics, and other subjects has been successful and makes more efficient use of the teacher's time. This device can be used successfully if the size of the groups is kept small: the individual approach must not be eliminated even in the group plan.

Clinical services have a unique contribution to make to the instructional program of the school. The degree of impact felt by the total program, however, varies with the role assumed by the specialist. Clinical programs are more effective if the specialist devotes less time to borderline clinical cases and more time to the role of consultant for all classroom teachers.

Auxiliary Services

Although the services for food, transportation, and maintenance are not usually considered a part of the instructional program, they do contribute much to it. These services have expanded over the past few decades and are now an integral part of most modern junior high schools. In many communities they are essential to maintaining equality in education for all boys and girls. Without them there would undoubtedly be more dropouts and the ideal of universal education would be further from realization.

Food services in the schools have expanded rapidly since the inauguration of support from relief funds in the 1930's. The National School Lunch Act of 1954 and later the School Milk Act encouraged schools to introduce food services and as a result the school lunch programs have expanded rapidly.

Although the actual work in the food services is in the hands of nonprofessionals, it is a responsibility of the educational authorities to administer this program as it is to administer other phases of the school program. The food program is operated with federal support and, as it is not a profit-making endeavor, the price of the services can be kept within the reach of all but a few boys and girls. Special provisions must be made for these few so that they will not be denied the services because of their inability to pay for them. Well-balanced meals in pleasant surroundings can contribute much to the educational program of the junior high school. A school lunch program can also conserve time that was formerly devoted to a lunch hour which, if long enough to provide time for pupils who lived a distance from school, was far too long for pupils who lived nearby or brought their lunches.

Transportation services have also grown rapidly with most states furnishing financial assistance to the local school as an incentive to reorganize into larger administrative units. The many small schools of a few years ago are now consolidating into large area schools that require transportation services. The city school system can usually arrange transportation through the public transit services. Smaller communities, however, must provide their own buses and operate their own transportation services. These, like the food services, fall under the direct supervision of the school.

Maintenance services are another facet of the total school picture that must be organized and administered by the school authorities. Custodial and repair personnel must be considered part of the educational team and must therefore be selected with care. These workers provide a physical climate within which an effective educational program can operate and their contributions should not be minimized. Although theirs is not considered a profession, they can be encouraged to think of themselves as craftsmen. This attitude, however, can be developed only if the professional personnel recognize their contributions.

Public Relations

A systematic development of sound relationships with parents and with the community as a whole is an essential part of any school program. Understanding on the part of the public is extremely important in the program of the junior high school, for many adults today are not products of a system that incorporated this type of program. The unique contribution of this newer school must be understood if the public is to support it to the extent that is necessary for its effective operation.

The organized public relations services of a junior high school may contribute publicity releases and use various outside-of-class activities to keep the name of the school before the public and—most important—interpret the program to the community. The highly commercialized athletic, music, and drama programs of many senior high schools are a constant source of publicity, but similar exploitation of the junior high school pupil can be seriously questioned. Furthermore, this superficial type of publicity does not elicit nearly so much school support as does a real understanding of the total educational program.

The publicity-type news release is much easier to produce than the informative release, but the value of the latter is incomparable. Newspapers are usually more interested in unusual or competitive events, but they will run feature stories on the educational program if the school prepares the basic information and furnishes an outline for such an article. But these stories are not forthcoming unless there is an organized attempt within the school to plan such releases.

The public relations program of a school is not confined to the news media. Again, careful planning is necessary if the total potential of the school is to be used in an over-all effort to explain the purposes of its various instructional and activity areas. Lay participation in the school is one of the better ways of promoting better understanding. If laymen are given the opportunity to work in certain school activities, they will have more interest in these activities. Too often, the PTA becomes a place for the parents to be entertained by the school rather than an opportunity for them to work with the school on some real educational problems. And laymen are excluded from many other projects of the school. It is true that uninformed parents can cause the school more trouble in working on a project than would be caused if the school worked alone. However, the uninformed but participating parent will soon become an informed parent who is willing to support the school more firmly.

Communication with the patrons of the school is another area that is often not too well planned. Bulletins to parents and brochures of general and specific information can add much to the public relations program, but these must be attractive and readable. Publications of this sort should come from the professional staff actively engaged in the instructional program. Bulletins explaining the purposes and activities of mathematics, for instance, should come from the mathematics teachers. Unfortunately, many teachers do not feel competent to produce materials of this sort and it is essential that they be given assistance in this task. The public relations service of the school does not necessarily prepare the releases, but it selects the ideas to be reported, provides help and encouragement in the preparation of releases, and arranges for their distribution. This service may be provided by the principal, by a special public relations department, or by a committee of teachers.

The hit-or-miss type of public relations program is not sufficient in our modern, complex society. The school must realize that it is in competition with many other agencies and commercial organizations for public support. If the school is to compete, it must have a well-organized service organization to see that the job is done in an efficient and effective manner.

Summary

Too often the classroom work of the school is considered the only important phase of the program. This is true in a sense, but if the various services of the school were suddenly withdrawn, the effectiveness of the instructional program would seriously diminish. The junior.high school deprived of the services of the library, guidance center, and audio-visual materials, would become a poor educational institution indeed.

Not all the many services found in various schools are necessary for an effective program, but each can contribute to the betterment of any school. Few schools can afford to employ all the desirable services to the full extent of their potentialities. Yet, partial services in most areas can be provided—on a part-time basis at least. Each school must study carefully the services that are desirable and then decide which can contribute most to the total instructional program.

CHAPTER VI

Evaluating and Reporting Pupil Progress

There is probably more dissatisfaction with the methods of evaluating and reporting pupil progress than with any other area of education today. This is evidenced by the fact that schools are constantly searching for more acceptable practices. Every few years a given school will reactivate its "report card committee" in an effort to find a better way to carry out this important task. Unfortunately, the revisions are often confined to the physical appearance of the report card: the old definitions are presented in different words.

The junior high school finds itself squarely in the middle of two conflicting ideas because of its position between the elementary school and the senior high school. Many elementary schools have replaced their report cards with parent-teacher conferences. Those retaining the report cards attempt to emphasize the performance of the child according to his ability rather than in relation to the achievement of the rest of his class. On the other hand, the senior high school is more and more under the domination of the college admission officers who demand a very strict academic evaluation that is highly competitive and based upon set standards of achievement. In this position, the junior high school finds its traditional function of providing a transition for the pupil from one philosophy of evaluation to another. This transitionary function, in this as in other phases of the junior high school program, requires a unique plan if it is to be accomplished.

Evaluating vs. Marking

Too often, the report card reflects the philosophy of grading that is found on the fruit farm. The small apples are placed in one basket; the blemished apples, in another; the rotten apples are thrown away; and the very best are carefully packed and sent to market. The farmer who merely grades his apples is doomed to failure. The intelligent farmer evaluates his crop to discover the cause of his inferior apples and takes measures to assure that next year's crop will have fewer rejects.

Marking pupils on a report card carries the same philosophy as grading apples. Marking is not necessarily evil, but unless it is considered as a small part of the total evaluation process, it contributes nothing to the educational program of a school. Very often the report card does extreme damage to both the very intelligent and the slow learner. The boy with a high academic aptitude can make an *A* without opening a book. Why then should he put forth an effort when the report card tells him he is doing all that is expected? On the other hand, the slow learner struggles along, working at the peak of his abilities, only to be faced with repeated failures on his report card. No wonder he becomes discouraged and leaves school before he is ready to assume his position in society. The American school system is based upon the premise that almost any youngster can have a secondary education if he will work for it. Too often the mark on the report card tells the superior child he can have it without effort and the slow learner that he is not good enough to claim the rights that the American people have demanded of him.

Parents of junior high school students usually demand report cards. But, this does not limit the school to reporting pupil progress in terms of marks alone. Marks can be given—but these should be accompanied by a total evaluation. This is not an easy task, but the teacher will be willing to put forth the effort required to make it a real educational experience for both the pupil and the parent.

The Parent-Teacher Conference

The parent-teacher conference has long been recognized by the elementary school as one of the more effective ways to report pupil progress. Its use in the secondary school, however, has been very limited because of the administrative organization. The self-contained classroom of the elementary school is easily adapted to the conference, for each teacher is primarily responsible for a single group and directs the major portion of all its learning activities. Thus, one teacher evaluates each pupil in all subjects and reports to his parents. The departmentalized organization of the junior high school presents a different problem: each pupil has several teachers and each teacher works with a number of different groups. Under this situation, a parent would have to have conferences with five or six teachers and each teacher would have to see well-over a hundred parents. It is obvious that a plan of this sort is not practical if the school expects to contact a high percentage of the parents.

One of the more commonly used plans for conferences in the junior high school is to hold an "open house." Teachers can be made available in their classrooms, and parents may go from teacher to teacher. Although this plan offers the opportunity for parents to see the teachers, it is not very effective in attracting many parents: general invitations to visit the school do not receive much attention on the part of parents. On the other hand, an invitation to visit a specific teacher at a specific time will usually bring a good response. This principle is probably the major factor in the success of elementary school conferences.

The most successful plan for conferences in the junior high school has been on the homeroom basis. In this plan, the homeroom teacher conducts the conferences and each parent is given a specific appointment. Some schools use this plan on a somewhat different basis: each teacher is assigned a group of advisees and conferences are held with the parents of the children assigned. In most cases the teacher acts as advisor to the same group for the entire three-year period. This gives the advisor time to get acquainted with the pupils and with their parents and to develop a long-range educational program.

It must be recognized that the parent-teacher conferences under the advisor plan must differ from those conducted by an elementary teacher in a self-contained classroom organization. The advisor does not have the pupil in all classes; in fact, he may not have the pupil in even one class. The conference must be based on the interpretation of report cards, standardized tests, and anecdotal reports from other teachers. In this situation, the parent has professional assistance in educational problems and the teacher assumes the role of an advisor. Very often the conference includes the parent, the teacher, and the pupil. Under this arrangement, the three act as a planning committee to chart the educational plans for the pupil. In case of difficulties, the advisor calls in the guidance counselor or some other specialist to help with the problems.

The advisory plan is a solution to many pupil-personnel problems. For example, the eighth-grader, going into the elective program of Grade 9, should have help in charting his educational courses. The parent, too, looks for help. The advisor, armed with the informative material from the school records, can do a great service in helping with the decisions. Figure 6–1 shows the registration form used at the State College High School, Cedar Falls, Iowa.

NINTH GRADE REGISTRATION

IOWA TESTS OF BASIC SKILLS - - PERCENTILE SCORES				
V Vocabulary	R Reading	L Language	A Mathematics	C Composite

Subject

☐ Algebra
(Above 50%ile on test A)

☐ General Mathematics
(Below 50%ile on test A)

☐ French 9
(Above 50%ile on tests V–R–L–C)

☐ Latin 9
(Above 50%ile on tests V–R–L–C)

☐ Industrial Arts

☐ Art

☐ Vocal

☐ Band

☐ Orchestra

☐ Science 9

☐ Social Studies 9

☐ Language Arts 9

☐ Home Economics

☐ Introduction to Business

☐ Physical Education and Health

Teacher Recommendations

Mathematics

Foreign Language

Industrial Arts
☐
Art
☐

Music
Vocal	Instrumental

Key to symbols under "Teacher Recommendations":

+ should be very successful in course
0 can be successful if willing to work hard
- lack interest and/or ability to be successful

Fig. 6–1.

This registration form is used by the advisor in helping the eighth-grader and his parent to select ninth-grade courses. Test scores are entered in the spaces provided and the recommendations of the eighth-grade teachers are placed in the spaces opposite the subject listings. In a parent-pupil-teacher conference of this sort, the advisor merely points out the test results and the recommendations of the teachers. With the use of this instrument, the able but lazy pupil finds it difficult to avoid taking a foreign language when both test results and teacher recommendations point to probable success. On the other hand, it is a much simpler matter for the teacher to suggest general mathematics if the child has low test scores in mathematics and is not recommended for algebra by his eighth-grade mathematics teacher. The advisor's recommendations are not based on opinion but upon objective test evidence and upon the recommendations of teachers who have worked with the pupil for a full year.

Parent-pupil-teacher conferences in the departmentalized junior high school can play a very important role in reporting to parents and in evaluating pupil progress in a manner that will be helpful and meaningful to both parent and child. A successful conference plan, however, is not easy to achieve and requires a strong and continuous in-service training program for the teachers. Such a program will bring reality to the frequent statement: "Every teacher is a guidance worker." Unless a teacher is given specific responsibilities for guidance work, she may never achieve enough competence to be effective in this important area of junior high school education.

The Use of Test Results

Both teacher-made tests and standardized tests are valuable tools in the total evaluative process. The act of administering a test is not necessarily an educative process but the use of the results of the tests can be educational. A standardized test imparts no information to the pupil, and unless the results are used to diagnose his situation it is better not to waste time in giving them.

One of the more frequent errors in testing is the failure of the school properly to interpret test results to the pupil and to his parents. This can be a difficult problem to solve, but the parent-pupil-teacher conference offers one of the best solutions yet devised for the junior high school. The junior high school pupil is capable of understanding the results of tests and their implications for his educational future. If the process of self-realization is to be developed, the adolescent must learn to evaluate his potentialities on the type of objective evidence furnished by test results.

Achievement tests have been proven over and over again to be better predictions of future educational success than any other type of test. The halo which for years surrounded the intelligence test has gradually faded. The intelligence test still provides some valuable information on the child, but care must be taken in interpreting the Intelligence Quotient. At best, the I.Q. is but an approximation of academic aptitude and variations in results from one test to another reflect that it is not an infallible instrument. Intelligence test results should be used to help the child understand himself. Most schools are willing to share the results of achievement tests with the pupils, but for some reason they keep the results of the intelligence test carefully concealed. If this bit of evidence is so important for the teacher in evaluation of the child, it would seem that it should be important to the child in evaluating himself. It is true that the I.Q. is not understood by the layman and is too often misinterpreted. Nevertheless, the results of the intelligence tests can be interpreted to the junior high school pupil in terms of the "academic aptitude" which it really represents. The I.Q. should be presented as a percentile—the increasingly accepted way of presenting all types of test results. The great secrecy surrounding the I.Q. stems from the early belief that the intelligence test was an absolute measure of a person's ability to do anything. Today it is recognized to be only an approximation of a person's ability to accomplish the verbal tasks that are commonly found in the academic subjects of the school. It is but another bit of evidence that can be used in the total evaluative process. But as long as it is concealed it cannot be used effectively.

One of the major mistakes in testing is the consideration of the results of one test in isolation from other evaluative information. A test often gives an inaccurate picture of an individual and there is danger in placing too much faith in the results of a single device. If the results of several tests and the evaluations of several teachers form a consistent pattern, a great deal of reliance can be placed on the total evaluation. The scattergram shown in Fig. 6–2, is one device that may be used in comparing two sets of test results. The vertical columns contain the names of pupils within given ranges of

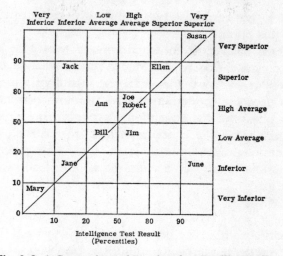

Fig. 6–2. A Comparison of Results of an Intelligence Test
and the Results of an Achievement Test.

intelligence test results. The horizontal columns contain names of pupils within certain ranges of achievement test results. It will be noted that in the lower lefthand square is one pupil (Mary) who has a very inferior rating in both the intelligence and the achievement tests. This is what we would normally expect. The diagonal line from lower left to upper right passes through the boxes where we would expect to find most of the pupils in a given class. Jack (upper left), however, has a low intelligence score but a high achievement score. June (lower right) has a high intelligence score but a low achievement score. It is obvious that there is an inconsistency in the results of the two tests. There may be several possible explanations and each must be examined carefully. It may be that Jack does have low academic aptitude but has worked hard and achieved far beyond what might normally be expected. On the other hand, one of the tests may have given an incorrect picture. It may be desirable to retest Jack or to compare these ratings with teacher evaluations.

Similar scattergrams can be made with test results on one axis and teacher marks on the other axis. In this sort of scattergram, the teacher will want to study carefully those pupils whose ratings are inconsistent and try to determine a true evaluation of the pupil. It must be recognized that there sometimes are inconsistencies between two valid ratings. This situation demands an explanation, however, and the alert teacher must re-examine her measuring devices as applied to this pupil.

Evaluations derived from teacher-made tests also need to be carefully examined. Poorly-constructed tests—whether commercial, standardized, or teacher-made—can give misinformation. There is a continuous need for in-service training in test construction as well as in other phases of the educational program. Both teacher-made tests and standardized tests are important tools in the evaluation of pupils. Their contribution to the total evaluative process depends on the particular tests given and on the wisdom with which the test results are used.

The Report Card

The report card has long been the most widely used link between the school and the home. Some authorities believe it is an outmoded device that had a place in the selective school of the past but is out of keeping in the school that is designed to educate all boys and girls. It is difficult to adjust a wide range of abilities to a single standard of achievement. On the other hand, many leaders in education support the use of the report card but usually urge its combination with other reporting devices.

One of the more serious criticisms of the report card is the inconsistency of the marks used to represent the evaluations. Seldom does a mark represent the traditional meaning: achievement on a strict academic basis. Instead, each teacher weaves into the mark a combination of achievement, attitude, and effort. The difficulty lies in the fact that no two teachers give the same weight to these various elements. One teacher may give much weight to effort while another may attach more importance to academic achievement. The result is that no one knows exactly what a *B* means. The attempt to mix the various elements into a single mark has resulted in a series of meaningless symbols.

It is becoming increasingly evident that to be meaningful, marks must reflect a single element. However, the junior high school teacher is taking part in the transition of boys and girls from the elementary school—which stresses achievement in relation to ability —toward the senior high school and college—where the premium is more and more on academic achievement. If both ideas are to be present on the junior high school report card, the answer does not lie in a single mark composed of both elements but in a dual marking system. One mark should represent achievement according to ability and the other should reflect achievement according to set standards.

The dual marking system offers some very definite problems that must be faced by a school introducing such a plan. There must be a careful consideration of the dual marks and plans must be made to insure that a proper balance is given to each. Actually, the mark representing achievement according to ability is much sounder from an educational point of view. Each child, regardless of ability, has an opportunity to realize his potential and to be recognized for that achievement. Parents, however, are accustomed to the marks of their own school days and will place more importance on the academic mark. Only with the face-to-face contact of the parent-teacher conference can the importance of each mark be explained.

If the junior high school is dedicated to the task of educating all boys and girls, it cannot use a report card that discourages or eliminates the slow learner and at the same time encourages laziness in the superior student who can reach minimum standards without effort. On the other hand, the parent and the pupil have a right to know where the pupil stands in the type of competitive achievement that will be faced in the senior high school and in college. A single mark based on a combination of two unrelated elements is not the answer to this problem. The only logical solution seems to be in the direction of a dual marking system with a proper balance in the value of the two.

Summary

Evaluation in the junior high school, as in other levels of the American school, cannot be on a limited base. Evaluation must be broad and must consider the many facets of the boy or girl being evaluated. Tests, both teacher-made and standardized, are important tools in evaluation but they are only a part of the total picture. Tests are relatively easy to use, but the danger in their use lies in the fact that they are not always as dependable as we would like them to be. Although a high degree of objectivity in evaluation is desirable, it must be recognized that there are many human traits for which we have no objective measurements. Many aspects must be evaluated subjectively, but with as much objective support as possible. In the final analysis, all the evidence collected—both objective and subjective—must be studied to find a pattern which will lead us to a total evaluation. A true evaluation cannot be reflected by a mark on a report card, so some other means of reporting pupil progress to the parents must be used. The most effective device that has been developed to date is the parent-teacher-pupil conference and it is most unfortunate that it is not used widely in the junior high school. The parent-teacher-pupil conference is a way for the junior high school to fulfill its commitments to its functions of guidance and helping in the transitional processes.

The unique position of the junior high school brings into focus two conflicting philosophies of marks and report cards. Both points of view have merit, but the two cannot be represented in a single, meaningful mark. If the two conflicting ideas cannot be resolved in actual practice, it would seem wise to move toward an acceptance of both but to keep them separated.

CHAPTER VII

Staffing the Junior High School

The importance of the teacher cannot be minimized. A quality school program depends upon competent and effective teachers. Although the physical aspects of the school plant—the equipment and the materials of instruction—are essential, they are of no value unless placed at the disposal of a good teacher. Even the monetary value of the teacher is recognized: 65–75 per cent of current expense budgets of most schools are allotted to teacher salaries.[1]

The staffing problems of the junior high school are generally similar to those of other levels in our school system, but there are a number of situations that create unique problems. These problems arise from the relative newness of the junior high school in the American education system and from its unique functions. Any new program in education will produce staff difficulties. The lack of organized training for a large number of teachers in a new area of education is always one of the major blocks in the progress of new ideas. Although the junior high school has established its unique role in education, there is still a definite lag in the preparation of teachers and in the numbers of individuals who look upon junior high school teaching as a career and plan their educational programs specifically for that level.

Teacher Education

At the outset of the junior high school movement, it was necessary to use teachers from either the elementary or secondary school. The low number of reorganized schools did not constitute a sufficient demand upon teacher education institutions to justify a curriculum especially designed for junior high school teaching. As more and more school systems reorganized to include separate junior high

---

[1] E. L. Morphet, R. L. Johns, and T. L. Reller, *Educational Administration: Concepts, Practices, and Issues* (Englewood Cliffs, N.J.: Prentice-Hall, Inc., 1959), p. 364.

schools, a few universities and colleges began to offer some special work in this area. Ackerman,[2] in a study of junior high school teacher education, found that few institutions give as much attention to the preparation of junior high school teachers as they do to the training of elementary and general high school teachers. His analysis also revealed that a majority of the programs offered were merely modifications of programs primarily designed for either elementary or general secondary school teachers.

The unique functions of the junior high school require a type of teacher education that is similar to existing programs but at the same time possesses features peculiar to this one specific level of education. The transitional role of the school demands a balance between the basic skills of the elementary school and the subject matter specialization of the senior high school. The teacher with an elementary school background endangers this balance, as does the teacher oriented to the senior high school program. At present there seems to be a growing trend toward the employment of secondary teachers, and the overemphasis on subject matter specialization is causing the junior high school program to become more and more a replica of the senior high school.

Another imbalance caused by the use of senior high school teachers is in the content of the specific courses. The intense specialization of senior high school teachers causes a serious problem in maintaining the general course concept that is so essential if the broad exploratory function of the school is to be realized. It is much easier to find a teacher of physics or of biology than it is to find a teacher of general science. Thus, the general science course in the hands of a physics teacher is likely to ignore or skim over the biological, chemical, and earth science experiences that are expected to be offered in the junior high school.

The 1960 Upper Midwest Regional Conference on Junior High School Education,[3] held at Cedar Falls, Iowa, recognized the lack of specific teacher education programs for the junior high school and made recommendations for improvement. They urged that such

---

[2] Ralph E. Ackerman, "A Critical Analysis of Programs for Junior High School Teachers in Teacher Education Institutions in the United States," *Bulletin of the National Association of Secondary School Principals*, Vol. 46, No. 271 (February, 1962), 394.

[3] *Bulletin of National Secondary School Principals*, Vol. 45, No. 266 (September, 1961), 18–48.

programs include courses in the teaching of reading, instruction in guidance, and information on conducting practical experience projects. It was felt that appropriate major-minor combinations, in addition to provisions for a broad general background, should be considered in the preparation of the teachers. The study of psychology, with emphasis on the adolescent, is considered essential, as are student-teaching experiences at the junior high school level. Along with these suggestions it was recommended that courses be included that meet the needs of the junior high school functions. These included instruction in reading methods, guidance, and appropriate junior high school techniques.[4]

In-Service Training

The evidence is clear that there is a definite deficiency in the preservice training of most junior high school teachers. This evidence points to an urgent need for a well-organized program of in-service training in the junior high school as well as throughout other levels of our school system. Not only must the junior high school keep teachers up-to-date and improve institutional practices, but it must actually retrain teachers for a role that has been neglected in their preservice preparation.

In a study of junior high school teachers in Texas, DeVane[5] found no evidence that any of the teachers had been specifically prepared to teach in the junior high school. If teachers have not prepared themselves for this level of teaching, it should follow that a very high percentage of them will not remain junior high school teachers. The validity of this reasoning is supported by Buddle, who found that junior high school teachers in Michigan were much less likely to remain in the field of teaching or at their grade level than were teachers at other levels of the school system.

If the junior high school is to attract and retain adequately trained teachers, the in-service training program must be designed to bring out the unique functions of the junior high school and to show that

---

[4] *Ibid.,* p. 32.

[5] L. M. DeVane, Jr., "The Qualities and Qualifications of the Excellent Junior High School Teacher," *Bulletin of the National Association of Secondary School Principals,* Vol. 46, No. 271 (February, 1962), 379–80.

this area of education has the professional possibilities of the older and more firmly established divisions.

Orientation of new teachers is a very important aspect of any in-service training program. It is doubly important in the junior high school if competent teachers are to be retained. The orientation will normally need to emphasize the unique problems of the junior high school, for a large portion of the newer teachers will probably not have had the specific preservice training for junior high school work.

Both orientation and continuous in-service training are necessary to keep the junior high school program in line with its accepted objectives. Some of the activities commonly used in such programs are:

1. Conferences and workshops that emphasize the junior high school point of view;
2. Visits to classrooms in local and neighboring schools where strong junior high school teachers are at work;
3. Cooperative efforts or team teaching with experienced junior high school teachers;
4. Curriculum study groups that continuously keep the philosophy of junior high school education in the foreground;
5. Summer school classes in junior high school education;
6. Proper supervision;
7. Faculty meetings that directly attack problems of the junior high school and make group decisions on the policy of the school;
8. The use of consultants on problems of junior high school education.

These and many other activities can help both the experienced and inexperienced teacher to grow professionally.

Selecting Teachers

Under ideal conditions, junior high school teachers would be selected on the basis of specific preservice training and upon successful teaching experience with junior high school boys and girls. It is obvious, however, that these criteria cannot always be followed in a field where few teacher preparation institutions offer the necessary work and where there is a definite lack of teachers continuing in junior high school teaching.

Because it is impossible to apply the usual criteria for teacher selection, it becomes necessary to develop new and more practical

criteria to meet the problems involved. Some of the points to consider in evaluating credentials of candidates could be:

1. Evidence of genuine interest in adolescent boys and girls as
shown by successful experience in camp work and organized recreational programs;
2. A broad background in general education;
3. A broad background in professional education, including
work in psychology;
4. A strong but broad background in the subject matter areas
(this would include double majors or a major and strong minor);
5. An interest in working at the junior high school level rather
than the feeling that it is a stepping stone to a senior high school
teaching position.

Very often these criteria, although difficult to judge objectively,
are just as important as the criteria of specific preservice training
and experience. A capable person with interest in his work can often
overcome the lack of specific training and become an outstanding
teacher in his new field.

Summary

The relatively new role of the junior high school in the American
educational system has not yet developed a volume of trained personnel commensurate with its needs. The lack of teachers in training
for specific work in junior high school education has made it rather
impractical for many teacher preparation institutions to offer a specific curriculum for this level. As a result, most junior high school
teachers must be recruited from the ranks of those who have been
trained for the elementary school or the senior high school.

This situation will be corrected only through the efforts of the
leaders in the field of junior high school education. The professional
possibilities should be presented to those entering the field of education and more appropriate programs should be encouraged in teacher
education institutions.

Until such time as there is an adequate supply of trained teachers,
the junior high schools themselves will have to assume the major
responsibility of orienting and retraining teachers to fit the needs of
the school. In-service training programs for junior high school staff
emphasis are essential. Not only is this type of program necessary
for the immediate improvement of instruction, but it is also a part

of a long-term program aimed at the retention of teachers in the school. Many good teachers, although trained for other levels of education, can be convinced of the professional opportunities of the junior high school if they are given the benefit of a good in-service program.

CHAPTER VIII

Forward Looking Practices

It is generally recognized that more scientific and technological advances have been made since World War II than were made throughout the history of mankind before that time. These advances and discoveries are placing a heavier load on the school, for the volume of knowledge is multiplied year after year and the schools are expected to keep pace. Another aspect of the increased tempo of development and experimentation in other phases of our society has effected the school. Not being content with the status quo, the teaching profession as a whole has become more experimentally minded and the schools are now confronted with new methods, materials, and devices that show definite promise for the improvement of instruction. Gradually, the technological advances of the scientific and industrial worlds are being adapted to use in the schoolroom: television, electronic computers, and automated instruction are becoming a normal part of school equipment.

Many of our newer approaches stem from the recent technological developments, but the majority of the educational innovations on the horizon today are based on knowledges and experiences of years past. They are just now beginning to attract attention because the atmosphere of our society demands that we move forward with newer and better instructional procedures—the school must keep up with the pace being set by other agencies in our society. Instruction materials and methods of presentation are changing at a rate that leaves the public school teacher in a position of adding the new tools of her trade or being left far behind.

Consideration is given here to but a few of the programs and movements that are beginning to make an impact on our schools. Some of these ideas are based on newer technological developments while others are older ideas that are just now being recognized as having merit in the newer demands that are being placed upon education.

Educational Television

The impact of television on American society cannot be minimized. There is little question of the impact of this medium on schoolchildren, to say nothing of its influence on the adult population. For a number of years there has been considerable interest expressed in the utilization of television for formal instructional purposes, but until recently very little had been done in this direction. In recent years, foundation grants have done much to promote the use of television. More recently, the U.S. Office of Education, under Title VII, Part B, of the National Defense Education Act of 1958, has begun to exert influence through investigation of possibilities and dissemination of findings.

Although much television instruction has been directed toward adults and out-of-school youth, study and experimentation is now being directed toward the use of television in the school situation. There seem to be some definite possibilities in the use of this medium to provide a broader range of experiences in the classroom than is possible when the instructional program must be restricted to the teaching personnel within a given school building. Programs of television instruction in areas where there are teacher shortages could contribute to a broader experience for the child. Television instruction in such subjects as foreign languages and science has been tried and has met with a degree of success. However, the type of television instruction that supplements the existing classroom program is more acceptable to our public schools than is the type which attempts to do the total instructional job with the regular teacher acting merely as a monitor.

One of the major strengths of television instruction is that the values of a superior teacher can be brought to a larger number of classroom situations. Few educators would dispute the idea that the superior teacher could do a more effective job in the actual classroom, but when we do not have enough of these teachers to cover all classrooms, television is one solution.

One of the criticisms of television instruction is based on its comparison with educational films. The question often asked is: Why cannot the television instruction be placed on film so that it could be used by the classroom teacher without rearranging the time schedule of the school to fit the television schedule? This argument does have merit and as time passes we may find that educational films are improved because of the impact of television. Films are usually segmented items which supplement the total instructional program. On the other hand, television instruction usually provides a series of experiences which are tied together in a logical sequence over a period of weeks—or even months. This sort of format for films could improve our classroom use of films and tie them into the total instructional program of a class.

The limited experience with television instruction has left many unanswered questions that are still being investigated. The junior high school would do well to watch the newer developments in this area, for they offer many possibilities in curriculum enrichment and provide opportunities to broaden the scope of general courses that are so important in the concept of junior high school education.

Out-of-Door Education

Out-of-door education has long been a part of the school program. Excursions to supplement the class program are commonly used by public schools and the school camp movement is growing rather rapidly. Camping as a part of the private school program originated over a hundred years ago and in 1912 the first public school venture in camping was recorded.[1] However, it has not been until recent years that out-of-door education has moved forward to any large degree. Michigan and California seem to have made more progress than other sections of the country but school camps are now beginning to appear in various parts of the United States.

Although many of the earlier school camping programs were a part of the elementary school program, more and more of the programs have moved into the secondary schools. The idea has not been widely accepted in the senior high school, but the junior high organization seems to be very adaptable to such a program and many successful junior high school camps are in operation.

Perhaps one of the major factors blocking the progress of public school camping is the idea that camping is largely a recreational activity that contributes very little to the classroom instructional program. It is unfortunate that many school camps have been pat-

---

[1] National Education Association, *Research Bulletin No. 4* (December, 1944), 153.

terned along these lines and have failed because of the lack of public support. It must be recognized that a school-sponsored camp cannot be justified on the basis of duplicating the experiences provided by summer camp programs of the various community agencies and private organizations. Such out-of-door programs do give many valuable experiences for young people but they do not provide the organized type of learning that classroom instruction offers. The public will support a school camp program only if the experiences can be tied into the curriculum of the school in such a way that they add to the existing instructional program.

If a junior high school camp program is to be successful, it should follow the philosophy and curriculum of the school itself. The activities of the camp must be a direct outgrowth of the classroom program and must make significant contributions to the learnings of the pupils. For example, a unit on geology or botany can be studied in the classroom, but for real meaning the pupils need to have access to an out-of-doors laboratory where specimens can be collected and identified in their natural environment. By the same token, a mathematics unit on indirect measurement or approximation of distances needs an out-of-doors laboratory where the principles of these units can be applied. Art and industrial arts find real meaning in appropriate out-of-doors experiences and the woods present some very unusual subjects for English compositions.

The out-of-doors experiences of the camp situation can be provided by several excursions spread over a longer period of time, but the camp offers an efficient administrative framework within which many of the excursion experiences can be offered during the one period of time and thus altering the regular school program as little as possible. Three or four days in a camp situation provides adequate time to offer many out-of-door experiences in all subject matter areas. The time limitations of the conventional school day do not interfere, as the pupils have twenty-four hours a day to engage in the activities.

The emphasis on supplementing the classroom work does not negate the possibilities of recreational activities in the camp. The longer instructional day provides ample opportunities for recreational activities and for the extraclass activities that are a traditional part of camp life.

The more successful school camps are operated on the principles of making the camp a school in the woods. Some of these principles are:

1. The school camp can be justified only on the basis of its contribution to the established instructional program.

2. Experiences in the camp should be those that are the most meaningful in the out-of-doors situation and experiences more adaptable to the classroom situation should be given in the classroom.

3. Some parts of the regular curricular courses should be offered in the camp curriculum.

4. The units of instruction should start in the classroom, move to the out-of-doors laboratory, and then return to the classroom for final analysis.

5. The regular classroom teacher should direct the learning experiences in both the classroom and in the camp. Outside resource persons may be used in both situations but the teacher should direct the total program.

6. Parents, pupils, and teachers should realize that the camp is a part of the regular school program. It is a serious but most enjoyable learning situation.

Programmed Instruction

Teaching machines and programmed instruction are among the later arrivals on the educational scene. These innovations have attracted considerable attention and hold much promise for the improvement of instruction at all levels. The principles behind this movement are not necessarily new but their application to the teaching process is.

The terms *teaching machines* and *automated instruction* caught the imagination of the American people and created much initial interest. The results envisioned were only somewhat short of magic but gradually it has been recognized that the so-called teaching machine is entirely dependent upon the instructional materials that are used in them. These programmed materials, rather than the mechanical device that displays them, have become the focus of attention. In fact, there has been a rather definite move toward the programmed textbook which presents the materials between the conventional bookcovers rather than placing them in a mechanical device. A number of research studies have shown no significant differences in learning between groups using programmed materials in book form and those using the same materials in a teaching machine.

The basic ideas for programmed instruction came from the laboratories of the behaviorist psychologists and are based on the following principles:

1. The learning task is broken into short, sequential, and logical steps.
2. There is a one-to-one ratio between the learner and the teacher (i.e., the program).
3. Each pupil actively participates in each step by making a response.
4. There is an immediate feedback to the learner so that he knows immediately whether or not his response is correct.
5. The learning steps are constructed so that there is a very high degree of success.
6. Each individual progresses at his own rate.

Although much interest has been shown in this new medium of instruction, there is definite opposition to it from many quarters, led by the Gestalt psychologists. The segmented, small steps of instruction are advocated by the learning theory of the behaviorist but are in direct conflict with learning by the whole method as advocated by the Gestaltist. The behaviorist feels that the logical sequence of the small steps in the program ties the learnings into a meaningful whole; the Gestaltist believes that an isolated bit of information has meaning only in relation to the total pattern.

Other persons argue that programmed instruction threatens to replace the teacher. These objectors argue that a good teacher with time to organize her instructional materials properly will do a much better job of teaching than a teaching machine. There is no doubt that this criticism is true, but the facts are that there are too few really good teachers and that in our present school situation the good teacher is usually not provided with enough time and materials to develop a consistently good total program of instruction.

Contrary to some of the early predictions for teaching machines, there is no danger of their replacing the teacher. Programmed instruction will undoubtedly assume its place in our schools as has the textbook, the film, and the many other media that have increased the efficiency of the classroom teacher. The classroom use of programmed materials will change the role of the teacher in the instructional program, but this change should be in the direction of providing more time for creative and original teaching.

The major problem involved in programmed instruction is finding the most effective ways to use it. The early materials were designed to accomplish the total instructional task. These self-contained programs attempted to offer a complete course or a complete unit of instruction. This trend seems to have turned in the direction of the multimedia approach. Under this concept, programmed materials are used for a portion of the presentation while textbooks, reference books, films, lectures, and a variety of other instructional media are used for the rest. Programmed instruction can be most effective when we can determine which portions of a given unit can best be taught with programmed materials and which portions are better explained through other media. Programmed instruction is a valuable contribution to education but there is still much work to be done in finding its most effective use.

Flexible Time Schedules

One of the major losses to Grades 7 and 8 when they became a part of the departmentalized junior high school was the flexibility of the time schedule. The effective elementary teacher, in a self-contained classroom, is able to deviate from her schedule with little difficulty. An elementary school teacher involved in a social studies discussion that has reached the stage of a real learning situation does not have to stop at the end of a given time to start an English lesson. Instead, she can extend her discussion into the English period and compensate for the time on another day. This is not true in a departmentalized organization of the junior high school. The teacher reaches a crucial point in a discussion and the bell rings. The discussion must stop because the pupils are scheduled to be in another room with a different teacher.

The Commission on the Experimental Study of the Utilization of the Staff in the Secondary School has presented plans to provide more flexibility in the scheduling of classes.[2] Although these plans do not offer a complete solution to the problem they do provide possibilities to improve the situation to a marked degree.

Present-day schedules of the junior high school are under the influence of the Carnegie Unit of Credit that has dominated the

---

[2] J. Lloyd Trump and Dorsey Baynham, *Guide to Better Schools* (Skokie, Ill.: Rand McNally & Co., 1961).

secondary schools since the early part of this century. The concept of the Carnegie Unit forces the curriculum builder to provide a course of instruction within a given time limitation. If there is more important material in the course than can be presented in one period a day, five days a week, then the materials must be cut down. If, on the other hand, the materials in another course do not need the standard allotment of time, then the course must be "padded" with unimportant materials. The logical pattern for curriculum construction would be to determine the important learnings to be achieved and then provide the time that is necessary to do the job. The concept of the Carnegie Unit prohibits this and as a result all classes meet for the same number of minutes each day without any reference to the relative importance of the subject matter.

The "block of time" plan that combines two courses in a double or triple period does provide some flexibility in the schedule but this is used only for a few classes in the junior high school and in cases where only one teacher handles both of the classes that are to be combined. Unrelated subject matter areas can have more flexible schedules by arranging them "back to back." An English class taught by one teacher can be scheduled to follow a social studies class taught by another teacher. On some days the social studies class could extend into the time for English and on other days the English class could use a portion of the time scheduled for social studies.

Another plan is to use short "modules" of time of about twenty minutes' duration. A given class would use two modules, or forty minutes, on certain days, while on other days three, four, or even more could be used. This plan involves some very complex scheduling problems but if there is improvement in the instruction it should be well worth the effort. The scheduling problems under such a plan may be substantially reduced by the use of electronic computers in scheduling. Considerable research is being conducted in the use of computers for this purpose and progress is being made. In a few years the junior high school can expect computer services for scheduling and other purposes to be available either within the school system or from area service units operated by universities or private organizations.

Team Teaching

Other recommendations of the Commission on Staff Utilization are team teaching and variations in the size of class groups. The broad and generalized courses of the junior high school demands both generalization and specialization on the part of the teacher. This combination is difficult to find; as a result, one element is usually sacrificed for the other. This problem could be solved, at least to some degree, by the use of more than one teacher for a given class. A broad social studies course could probably be more effectively taught by three teachers. Each of these teachers would be assigned to teach the unit for which she is best qualified. One teacher with a broad background in sociology could form a team with two other teachers with backgrounds in history and in economics or government. As a team, this group could do a much more effective job. Another team could be composed of a master teacher, regular teachers, and teachers' aides. The master teacher could present materials to a large group and then break the large group into smaller groups under the other team members for discussion and individual help.

Variations in class size should be studied carefully by junior high schools even though the team approach is not in use. There is no magic in the number of thirty or thirty-five as a maximum class size. This is an element that should be decided by the nature of the class. Some classes could probably be taught effectively with forty or fifty pupils while others should have fewer than twenty. It seems logical that much time could be saved by a teacher if she did not have to repeat herself four or five times each day. Certain presentations could be made to five sections at one time. The time saved by the teacher could be devoted to smaller groups to attend to individual differences. Again, the problem of scheduling the various-sized groups for different learning situations presents some administrative problems. It can be done, but it is extremely complex. With the aid of the electronic computer, these problems may be solved and this sort of scheduling could become commonplace.

The Ungraded Junior High School

The ungraded elementary school idea has attracted considerable attention but only a few attempts have been made to apply the concept to the secondary school.[3] In reality, the ungraded concept does exist to some degree in the elective programs of the departmentalized secondary school and this could very easily be expanded to provide an ungraded organization. The pattern of requiring all pupils, regardless of ability, to take a certain sequence of courses is questionable. Many boys and girls could profit much more from three years of seventh-grade level English than they do from progressing through the regular sequence of English courses now offered. On the other hand, a boy with a high aptitude for mathematics could easily be doing some very advanced mathematics before the end of Grade 9 if the administrative structure permitted him to do so.

Every junior high school class will have pupils who could profitably skip certain basic courses and advance to others that offer a greater challenge. This would not necessarily mean that junior high school could be completed in less than three years, but it could mean that more electives could be offered so that the superior pupil could have a richer program, not only of academic courses, but also of the fine and practical arts that he often misses under our present organization.

The concept of the ungraded school differs from the idea of ability grouping. Ability grouping administratively forms a higher level group of pupils and places them in the fixed sequential pattern that we have always had in our schools. The ungraded concept provides for each individual to be placed in a situation that most nearly fits his needs. Individual scheduling of each pupil would seem to offer a much better solution to meeting individual differences than the practice of placing a pupil in a group that keeps step through three years of school.

The Learning Laboratory

The study hall has disappeared from many junior high schools but there is still a problem of providing a time and place for independent study. It is no mystery that the study hall has been looked upon with disfavor in many circles. In too many cases it is a "guard" hall rather than a "study" hall. Actually, it has often been used as

---

[3] B. Frank Brown, "An Ungraded Secondary School," *Bulletin of the National Association of Secondary School Principals*, Vol. 45, No. 246 (April, 1961), 349f.

an administrative device to store away pupils who are not scheduled for a class in the hope that they will do some sort of constructive work. The use of the library during study hall periods does provide a general type of learning laboratory but the general laboratory with a general type of guidance is not nearly so effective as a specialized laboratory with specialized guidance.

The science laboratory has been in use for many years in the junior high school as a place for classwork. Little attention, however, has been given to a science laboratory that can be used by the pupil for independent work during study period. Today's foreign language laboratory is likely to lose its effectiveness if it cannot be used at times other than language class periods. In a similar manner, the machines in a business education laboratory should be made available at times other than class periods so that students may practice the skills they have developed in their typewriting classes. The learning laboratories in such areas as language arts, mathematics, and social studies offer some distinct possibilities but little has been done to explore them. There is little question that independent study time could be made very profitable if taken out of the conventional study hall and placed in an administrative structure of learning laboratories.

Other Innovations

The rapid growth in the volume of educational ideas places every junior high school teacher and administrator in the difficult position of keeping up with new developments and adapting them to his school. The many new types of projectors and recorders would offer priceless aids to efficient instruction. Newer and faster methods of producing teacher-made materials is another area in which we are finding valuable contributions. The use of telephone amplifiers that can bring a U.S. Senator or a famous poet into the classroom for a private conversation offers many possibilities for making the classroom situation more meaningful.

New ideas are surrounding the profession today, and it is the obligation of the professional worker to keep abreast of these developments and to learn how they can be used most effectively. A medical doctor who does not keep up with newer developments in his field cannot hope to maintain his practice. A disease that was incurable last month may have a very simple cure next week. We expect our doctors to know about the newer developments. By the same token, the public has a right to expect the teachers of the junior high school to know about and use the many new developments in education.

CHAPTER IX

Issues in Junior High School Education

There is a wide range of diversified practice in the junior high school today. The differences are based upon conflicts in philosophies and traditions, and the lack of careful analysis of the school situation. Whenever a controversy arises, supporters from both sides muster their forces and state their respective points of view in the educational literature. One can find a sufficient volume of support in educational literature to back any point of view one wishes to take. To a visitor who comes to the United States from a country with a strong centralized school system, our situation appears to be one of utter confusion. However, it is this element of confusion that has fostered one of the greatest educational systems that the world has ever seen. (Even the foregoing statement is one of controversy, for many persons feel that our schools should return to the European pattern from which we started in the seventeenth century.) Even the critics of our schools who, in the post-Sputnik era, advocated a return to the highly selective plan to raise standards through the elimination of the child with lesser academic aptitude, made a definite contribution to the existing American school system. Under the fire of these criticisms the standards of academic achievement reached new heights—but not through the elimination of the poorer student. Instead, by renewing his efforts, the professional educator was able through better organization and improved instruction to raise the academic standards for the superior student and at the same time to make better provisions for the slower student. Instead of turning to the idea of selectivity in the junior and senior high schools, there was a renewal of the faith of the American people in the principle that *all* American youth could be served more effectively in a single school that provided opportunities for children at all levels of ability than in different schools designed for different levels of ability and denying the opportunity of a secondary education to a large block of youth.

Controversy provides for a careful analysis of educational practices. If all aspects of the controversy are thoroughly aired, the chances are that the American schools will soon reorganize the unsound arguments, and establish practices that are based on an intelligent diagnosis of the situation. This is not to say that there is a wrong side and a right side to our professional disagreements. Instead, there are usually valid reasons to support either side. When all the evidence is assembled, however, a value judgment must be made in favor of the position that seems to have the most advantages. In some cases a compromise is reached in which the desirable aspects of both sides are combined into a workable solution.

Many of the controversies of the junior high school today are gradually reaching the point where enough evidence is assembled on both sides so that a professional worker can begin to make value judgments and direct his efforts toward a satisfactory solution. Some of the prominent issues of today are considered here and a point of view is expressed. These may not be views acceptable to the reader but they do provide some evidence that will eventually lead to a solution.

Vertical vs. Horizontal Enrichment

The school of a few decades ago practiced double promotions and retention as matters of course. Later we came through the period of social promotions that insured advancement each year and made no provisions for early completion of the school sequence. Gradually techniques were developed so that individual differences could be provided for at each grade level through remedial work for the slow pupil and enriched experiences for the better student.

Retention and grade-skipping are administrative devices designed to reduce the range of individual differences in the classroom. Enrichment is an instructional technique designed to raise the level of the slow pupil and at the same time push the fast learner further ahead. In reality, this concept actually increases the range of individual differences in a given grade. Gradually, this process has come to be recognized as good educational practice.

The problem now under question is not one of enrichment as opposed to nonenrichment but of determining the nature of enrichment. Should the superior pupils in the seventh grade be restricted to an area of instruction reserved for that grade but be directed into a deeper study of it? On the other hand, should the superior seventh-grader be moved on to study the materials and content of the eighth grade? Neither seems to be a logical answer to the problem but a combination of both could be a solution. Horizontal enrichment—going deeper into a given area—is an important part of the total program for the superior pupil, but such a process can easily be carried to an extreme. Many pupils can dig more deeply into a given area and still have time to advance upward into new areas, and provisions should be made for this type of program.

The departmentalized nature of the junior high school permits both horizontal and vertical enrichment. Pupils can move forward and at the same time do so on a very broad base. Quite often an eighth-grader could get much more benefit from a ninth-grade mathematics class than from staying with his eighth-grade group. This does not necessarily mean that he is headed toward early graduation from high school, but—by skipping some of the basic courses in the junior high school—he could have time for more electives that would provide a broader educational base. The real issue in enrichment lies in the administrative organization that demands that a pupil must be a full-time eighth-grader or a full-time ninth-grader, thus permitting either vertical enrichment or horizontal enrichment but not both.

Ability Grouping

Conant's report on the senior high school[1] was influential in stimulating the use of ability grouping. His recommendations, based on the opinions of many educators, were very favorable to ability grouping as long as it is done on a subject-by-subject basis. He advocated grouping in accordance with performance in each subject area. Thus, a pupil could be in a superior group in English but in an average or low group in science.

Considerable research has been conducted in the area of ability grouping, but there is no evidence to show that ability grouping increases achievement as measured by standardized achievement tests. Controlled experiments have not shown that the average pupil in an average group achieves any higher than the average pupil in an ungrouped situation. The same is true for pupils of high and low ability. It is recognized, however, that standardized tests do not

---

[1] James B. Conant, *The American High School Today* (New York: McGraw-Hill Book Co., Inc., 1959).

measure all the desirable outcomes of education and many educators feel that the unmeasured elements in the group situation are of sufficient benefit to justify the practice. Teachers who handle the superior and average classes seem to favor ability grouping, but the teacher with the low-achieving group usually does not share their enthusiasm.

Ability grouping is but another device to reduce the wide range of individual differences that exists in a given classroom. For the teacher who is not able to provide for individual differences, this device probably has some merit but the skillful teacher can and does take care of individual differences in either a grouped or ungrouped situation. There is little objective evidence to support ability grouping nor is there objective evidence to show that it is detrimental. If an educator bases his decision upon objective evidence, there is no reason why he should or should not use ability grouping. It does cause some complications in the traditional marks on the report card but there have always been problems in this area and the new problems do not make the situation any worse than it is already.

The strange situation in the area of providing for individual differences is that we do have objective evidence to support other methods, but these are seldom considered. A number of very carefully controlled experimental situations have produced evidence to show that the use of differentiated assignments and a variety of materials in the classroom do produce a significantly higher degree of learning as measured by standardized tests. The truth is that the school attempts to solve a very important problem with an administrative structure such as ability grouping when the real solution lies in an in-service training program that helps the teachers learn how to provide for individual differences in either a heterogeneous or a homogeneous group.

Administrative Organization

The administrative organization of the American school system started with the 8–4 structure. As the junior high school movement started, the trend was toward the 6–2–4 plan. Gradually this plan shifted to the 6–6 organization which is the most common today, but there has been a rapid growth in the 6–3–3 plan as enrollments have increased. It appears that this trend toward the 6–3–3 organization will grow as population growth increases the number of pupils entering secondary schools and as the consolidation of smaller districts creates larger community schools. The factors which exert the most influence seem to be those of administrative expediency. Such items as size of enrollment, size of buildings, and existing facilities are the major considerations. The planning of new buildings and new facilities to take care of increased enrollments is increasing the trend toward the 6–3–3 plan. In some situations the decisions are dominated by local laws. For example, Illinois law encouraged a township high school organization of four years with a complete separation from the lower eight grades. The two divisions operate independently with separate boards of education and separate superintendents. Organizations of this type offer little opportunity for a choice between various plans and neither the 6–6 nor the 6–3–3 organization can be attempted unless the entire legal structure of the school is changed.

Some research on the relative merits of the 6–6 and 6–3–3 plans has been completed but most research to date has compared the 8–4 plan with the various reorganized plans. There is little objective evidence to support either the 6–6 or 6–3–3 plans. Opinion surveys of administrators, teachers, parents, and pupils, however, usually show a preference for the 6–3–3 plan.[2]

There seem to be some very definite advantages for each of the two organizational patterns and a particular school must base its decision on the particular situation in that school. In the case of a large enrollment, it may be much more desirable to operate a junior high school which is physically removed from the senior high school. The small school, however, must weigh the advantages of keeping the various age levels separate against an improved instructional program. It is difficult for a small junior high school to justify equipment and rooms that may be used only two or three periods a day. The facilities could be justified if they were shared with the senior high school. It would be rather expensive for a small junior high school to offer such subjects as typewriting, home economics, and industrial arts if separate facilities had to be maintained. Staff utilization is also much more flexible in a six-year school than in a

---

[2] Jerald L. Reece, "The Three-Year Junior High School vs. the Six-Year Junior-Senior High School," *Bulletin of the National Association of Secondary School Principals,* Vol. 46, No. 271 (February, 1962), 23–38.

separate junior high school. The problems of staff assignments, however, are reduced as the size of a school increases. This presents a minimum of difficulty in the very large three-year junior high school.

In most six-year schools an effort is made to separate many of the extraclass activities and, whenever possible, the junior and senior high schools are housed in separate sections of the building. But the idea of providing the best possible program for early adolescents is often confused with the mechanical act of segregating them from older children. The association of younger children with senior high school students may be bad in certain activities but under other conditions it could result in advantage for both groups. Each school must weigh the evidence and make a decision based on what will contribute most to the total educational program.

Interscholastic Athletics

Probably no other single controversy in junior high school education attracts more public attention than the issue of competitive athletics. Any significant list of recommendations for the junior high school is examined by the press to discover the stand taken on interscholastic competition, and newspaper headlines emphasize that phase of the report while other recommendations are skimmed over. It is most unfortunate that so much time is spent on problems of little importance when real issues are at stake.

Either side of the athletics issue may be supported, but even a mild emphasis on interscholastic athletics at the junior high school level is questionable. The values claimed for interscholastic competition can be achieved by a well-rounded intramural program and in such a program the benefits are felt by a higher percentage of the student body.

The evidence against interscholastic competition is not conclusive enough to say that it is altogether bad. However, the school that does offer this type of activity should first be sure that it is taking care of the total school population through a well-organized physical education program and a well-rounded intramural program. The physical education program should be on a regular basis and under the direction of teachers who emphasize activities other than seasonal sports. The seasonal sports emphasis may be left to the intramural program. When these two elements of the program are operating at a high level, the school may then consider the pros and cons of a limited interscholastic program. But the junior high school that goes into an interscholastic program before the generalized instruction is operating effectively is violating one of the basic functions of the school and may expect to be criticized.

Regional Accreditation

The inspection and accreditation of the junior high school by the local state departments of public instruction has been a rather universal practice for many years. Many junior high schools, however, have expressed an interest in accreditation by the various regional associations that accredit colleges and secondary schools. The original purpose of the accrediting associations was to promote a better understanding and articulation between the high school and college. Later the functions expanded to increase the standards of excellence of all its member schools, colleges, and universities.

The North Central Association of Colleges and Secondary Schools, which was organized in 1895 and operates in nineteen states of the North Central area of the United States, does accredit Grades 7, 8, and 9 when they are a part of a six-year high school. However, a six-year high school is not required to include these grades, and there is no provision for accreditation of separate junior high schools by the Association.

A study conducted by the Association in 1961 revealed considerable support for accreditation of the junior high school.[3] The schools surveyed were larger schools and about 72 per cent were organized as three-year high schools. Both superintendents and principals of these schools were asked to express their opinions on accreditation; 66 per cent of the principals and 62 per cent of the superintendents favored such a plan. Approximately 20 per cent of both superintendents and principals opposed accreditation by the North Central Association. A number were undecided. The study also revealed that school officials, who favored moving slowly into a regional accreditation program, felt that policies and guidelines for

---

[3] Stephen A. Romine, "Opinions About North Central Accreditation of Junior High Schools," *North Central Association Quarterly*, Vol. 25, No. 2 (Fall, 1961), 193–200.

accreditation should be developed specifically for junior high schools.

The Southern Association of Secondary Schools and Colleges began the accreditation of junior high schools in 1954. The Association has also been working to improve elementary schools. In 1959, the Association authorized accreditation of elementary schools and accrediting began the following year. Elementary schools are not taken into full membership but are only affiliated with the Association.

There is some concern among junior high school people over the possibility of the accreditation of their schools by the regional accrediting associations. These persons point out that the original function of these agencies was to promote articulation between the high school and college. It is feared that affiliation with such an agency would lead the colleges to dominate the junior high school curriculum. The junior high school has enjoyed a degree of freedom from the pressures of college preparation and many persons would resist any movement that endangers this freedom.

In actual practice, the regional associations are voluntary organizations that have no legal status. A school may join, or not, as it wishes. There is a certain amount of prestige involved for the schools that can meet the requirements for membership and very often this prestige factor is almost mandatory as far as the administration of the school is concerned.

The North Central Association is organized into different commissions. The Commission on Secondary Schools is separate from the Commission on Colleges and Universities, with the member schools of a particular commission having the right to impose rules and regulations only in their commission. The college domination of the Association is actually a misconception when one realizes that the Commission on Secondary Schools in 1962 included over 3600 schools while the Commission on Colleges and Universities totaled only 457 schools.[4] It is obvious that any question coming up before the combined commissions could not be dominated by the colleges.

It seems that voluntary membership in an accrediting association is desirable for the junior high school movement. A uniform list of minimum standards could do much to improve the junior high

---

[4] *North Central Association Quarterly,* Vol. 37, No. 1 (Summer, 1962).

schools as a whole and the continued encouragement of the association for the member schools to move forward would be very helpful.

There are many advantages to be gained by the affiliation of the junior high school with one of the existing associations. However, those who fear this affiliation may have a sound basis for the organization of a different set of accrediting agencies with no connection with the ones now operating for the colleges and secondary schools. The advantages of a voluntary accrediting agency are obvious and the junior high school movement would receive much more recognition if it organized such an agency or affiliated with the existing ones.

Merit Pay

Salary increases for outstanding performance is an issue that is attracting much attention at all levels of education. The pros and cons of this issue are presented in almost every professional publication. Teacher organizations such as the National Education Association and the American Federation of Teachers have brought up the issue over and over in their meetings. The many arguments on both sides may be reduced to two statements. Those favoring merit pay claim it is desirable and that it should be adopted so that adequate evaluative devices can be developed and tested to determine those entitled to merit pay. Persons opposing merit pay usually agree that the principle is good but it is not practical because teaching proficiency cannot be adequately evaluated.

It seems that in a situation where there is common agreement on the desirability of a practice, every effort should be made to place it in effect. It is an established fact that mistakes will be made in the evaluation of teaching effectiveness and some undeserving teachers will receive merit pay while some of the better teachers may be overlooked. However, it is also a fact that inequity exists in a salary schedule that does *not* consider teacher effectiveness. Such a salary schedule is geared to the average teacher and inequities are evident in the salaries for both the good and the poor teacher. On the other hand, under a merit pay plan, there will be very few mistakes made in the evaluation of the outstanding teacher because she can be easily identified. The same is true for the poor teacher. There may be some mistakes made in the evaluation of the average group, but with systematic evaluative procedure, the number of these mistakes could be reduced. A careful analysis of the situation will reveal that fewer mistakes in setting salary will be made under a merit plan than under a uniform plan that applies the same salary scale to all.

There seems to be little question that fewer mistakes will be made in a situation in which a real effort is made to evaluate than in a situation where no such attempt is made.

Homework

The question of homework is a problem that is always present in the junior high school. It is not uncommon to find a policy of no homework in the elementary school. Even schools which assign homework at this level usually keep it to a minimum. On the other hand, few senior high schools place restrictions on homework assignments. This situation places the junior high school in its natural role of a transitional school.

Research in the area of homework offers very little toward a solution of the problem, for there is considerable conflict in the findings. Some experimental studies have shown a difference in achievement between groups which are given homework assignments and groups which are not; other studies have shown no significant differences. The same conflict is shown by surveys of parent opinion on the subject. Some parents feel that homework at the junior high school level is essential while others ask that school time be provided for independent study.

The general pattern in junior high schools has been to make some homework assignments, and with the advent of Sputnik and the drive for academic excellence, this practice has been accentuated. Most junior high schools now provide some sort of homework assignments, which tend to increase each year as the pupil advances toward senior high school.

Some junior high schools, following the pattern of many senior high schools, have moved toward longer class periods with the idea that some of the classroom time would be devoted to supervised study. This plan has helped, in some degree, to reduce the pressure of long homework assignments, but as time advances, most schools on this plan find the teacher taking more and more of the longer period for instructional purposes and not leaving class time for individual work.

The departmentalized structure of the junior high school complicates the problem of homework, as it is not uncommon for a pupil to receive several heavy assignments one day and very few the next. This coupled, with the extraclass activity program, can very easily place pupils under undue pressure from time to time. Planning for the coordination of homework assignments in a departmentalized organization is most difficult and can easily reduce the flexibility that a teacher needs in making such assignment to fit into the instructional sequence.

The more fruitful efforts have been in attempts to improve assignments rather than to determine their length or pattern. The concept of out-of-class assignments is a broader idea than the homework assignment. Too often "homework" is restricted to paper and pencil tasks or definite reading assignments that require no special facilities. The out-of-class assignment includes these elements but also works in the laboratory, the library, and other resource centers. It may also include interviews with persons in the school and in the community, visits to various places of interest, and events of educational value. This broader concept of assignments can make for more meaningful assignments with a variety that will take the drudgery away from such activities and make them enjoyable regardless of the time necessary to complete the task.

Summary

Controversy is the keystone upon which the American educational system was built. The principle of local control in our public schools has provided an atmosphere in which professional educators can disagree and put into practice various plans that are in opposition. This gives all schools an opportunity to study and to select practices that have been tried in actual classroom situations. In fact, the freedom to take a point of view and test its effectiveness has stimulated the largest amount of informal research in education that the world has ever seen.

Educational journals and books today are filled with accounts of practices that have been used with success in different schools. Not all are successful when transplanted into other schools and very often controversies arise when one school finds a practice successful and another school finds it unsuccessful. It is recognized that many aspects of education cannot be proven by controlled experimentation because of the lack of accurate measuring instruments. Where objective evidence can be produced, we should consider it. But in other cases we must rely upon value judgments in which the pros and cons are carefully weighed and a subjective decision is made.

The junior high school teacher today must keep abreast of new practices and carefully study their pros and cons. Each school must make decisions as to the direction in which it will go. Broad reading and careful investigation is necessary if wise decisions are to be made. Every professional teacher has an obligation to study the issues and arrive at a personal decision that will lead to the adoption of a particular practice. Some mistakes will be made, but, in the long run, the junior high school education will be better served if decisions are made upon which positive action can be based.

CHAPTER X

Evaluation of the Junior High School

Much time and effort is expended in the evaluation of junior high school pupils but very often the faculty of the school does not spend enough time in an evaluation of the educational program itself. It is true that an assessment of pupil growth in a particular school is a good indication of the program, but this is only a portion of the total evaluative process. It must be recognized that pupil growth must not be measured by the same standards in all schools. The suburban junior high school that serves a high-level economic and cultural group would expect to have pupils with a high average academic aptitude. In such a situation the pupil growth will probably be above average even if the school program is not operating as well as it should. On the other hand, an excellent instructional program in an underprivileged community will have difficulty showing an average growth. The community, the school, the pupils, and many other factors must be considered in a total evaluation.

Evaluation of the school is aimed, of course, at improvement of the effectiveness of the program. The processes of improvement usually follow the standard three-step procedure of (1) identification of strengths and weaknesses, (2) diagnosis of the causes of strengths and weaknesses, and (3) corrective measures to strengthen the weak aspects of the program. Actually, this three-step process is the total picture of evaluation. Evaluation improves instruction only when the entire cycle is completed. Identification of a problem has little value unless steps can be taken to correct it.

Standardized Tests

The most commonly used tool in the evaluation of the instructional program is the standardized achievement test. The results of these tests indicate relative achievement in the various academic areas when compared to national norms. Although achievement test results may be used effectively, care should be exercised in their in-

101

terpretation. Test results must be interpreted in terms of the total school situation if they are to be of value in the identification of weaknesses and strengths. The philosophy of the school should be consistent with the philosophy of the test constructors if the results are to be meaningful. For example, the instruction of an English department that does not believe in stressing formal grammar should not be evaluated by a test that emphasizes the parts of speech, formal sentence construction, and rules of grammar. Low scores in a situation of this sort merely reveal a difference in philosophy and not a deficiency in the instructional program. The same is true in other areas. A test based on conventional mathematics will not measure the growth in modern mathematics.

Another misuse of test results occurs in the practice of drawing conclusions from a single test. The profile of a given class for a single year is but a comparison of that class with others at the same grade level all over the United States. One of the more important comparisons should be made between the scores of an eighth-grade class and the scores that same group made as seventh-graders. Growth is the most important aspect of evaluation, and one test is not enough to reveal growth. Two forms of the same test given a year apart will indicate the growth factor. An eighth grade that shows an average performance on a test may or may not have shown a growth pattern. If the group was well below average in the seventh grade, then an average score at the eighth grade would indicate a desirable trend. However, if the ninth grade results show average performance while the same group in the eighth grade had a higher than average performance, there is an indication that something is wrong either with the test or with the instructional program.

Too often performance on tests is used by the administration for evaluation of teachers or for publicity purposes. Both practices are questionable unless other aspects of the school program are included in a total evaluation. It must be remembered that the basic skills of a class are reflected in the results of any academic test. A class with a poor background cannot hope to achieve high test results even after a few months with a superior teacher. By the same token, a school in a high-level economic and high cultural community is being unfair when it publicly compares its test results with those of schools in underprivileged communities.

Follow-up Studies

The follow-up study has long been an important part of the senior high school evaluative program. However, it has not been used to an influential degree in junior high schools. Many problems of the junior high school could be identified if a systematic and continuous follow-up study were made. A comparison of the performance of former junior high school students in the senior high school could uncover strengths and weaknesses in the junior high school instructional program, or could reveal a difference in the philosophy of the two schools. In either case, the problems could be identified and a cooperative effort made to correct the situation.

Dropouts in the senior high school can often be traced to causes in the junior high school, and corrective steps can and should be taken at the level where the difficulties begin.

One of the more important results of the junior high school follow-up study could be a closer working relationship between the teaching staffs of the two schools. Too often, the horizontal curriculum development of a given school would be improved if the vertical aspects of curriculum planning could be expanded both upward and downward to include the entire school system. The junior high school finds itself in a situation to work upward with follow-up studies and to work downward with reports to the elementary schools that furnish the pre-junior high school experiences.

Self-Evaluation

The concept of self-evaluation is based on the premise that if a person discovers his own inadequacies he is more likely to take steps to correct the deficiencies. This is a sound principle and one that should be used in the evaluation of the school program. There is one major difficulty in such a plan and that is the danger involved in a school's resorting to unsound rationalization when an evaluative process uncovers questionable practices. It is very easy for a school to claim, when test results are low, that the test was not in accordance with its philosophy. This should have been determined before the tests were selected and administered to the pupils.

Although the idea of self-evaluation is good, it should be combined with some sort of external controls that will prevent the school from looking only at the favorable aspects of their programs and ignoring less favorable ones.

Probably the most broadly used plan of school evaluation is the *Evaluative Criteria*[1] developed through a cooperative effort of the five regional accrediting associations in the United States. This device structures a systematic and thorough approach to all aspects of the school program, including a study of the community and the administrative structure of the school as well as the instructional program itself. It combines the self-evaluation principle with an external inspection that either confirms or revises the evaluation made by the faculty of the school. Although this device is designed for the total secondary school, it can be used by the junior high school. It has been used broadly by the various regional accrediting associations in the evaluation of member schools. Normally, a school faculty first carefully evaluates the various aspects of its program. Then a team of visitors spends two or three days in the school going over the self-evaluation forms and checking them against the practices that are evident while the school is in operation.

In 1962, the General Committee of the National Association of Secondary School Principals authorized a study to determine the need for evaluative materials for the junior high school. The proposal of modifying the 1960 edition of the *Evaluative Criteria* for the junior high school met with enthusiastic response from the various state supervisors of secondary education and this plan was adopted. The machinery was immediately set into action for a 1963 publication of evaluative criteria specifically designed for the junior high school.[2]

Another device, designed exclusively for the junior high school, is the *Utah Junior High School Evaluative Criteria*. This device also provides for both self-evaluation and an evaluation by a visiting committee. This instrument was developed through a cooperative effort of the Utah Secondary School Principals' Association, the Utah State Department of Public Instruction, and the National Association of Secondary School Principals.[3]

---

[1] National Study of Secondary School Evaluation, *Evaluative Criteria* (Washington, D.C.: The National Study of Secondary School Evaluation, 1960).

[2] Roderic C. Matthews, "Evaluative Criteria for Junior High Schools," *Bulletin of the National Association of Secondary School Principals,* Vol. 46, No. 276 (October, 1962), 111–13.

[3] J. Lloyd Trump, "Two Instruments for Evaluating Junior High Schools," *Bulletin of the National Association of Secondary School Principals,* Vol. 44 No, 259 (November, 1960), 130–32.

Another device of the same nature was developed by the Oklahoma Curriculum Improvement Commission and sponsored by the Oklahoma State Department of Public Instruction.[4] Still another instrument designed to include both self-evaluation and an external evaluation was developed by William G. Anderson.[5] This device guides the staff through an evaluation of eight categories of the school program: (1) philosophy, (2) staff, (3) student population, (4) the setting of the school, (5) curriculum, (general), (6) curriculum, (specific), (7) co-curriculum, and (8) student services. The plan of evaluation is developed in three phases: Phase I: An Inventory; Phase II: Self-Evaluation; and Phase III: An Active Program for Improvement. These three phases embody the fundamental principles that must underlie any effective evaluation.

Summary

A complete and meaningful evaluation of a junior high school program must embody three distinct yet interrelated steps. These are:

    1. A survey of the existing program and its relation to the community it serves.

    2. An evaluation of existing practices to identify both the weak and the strong aspects of the program.

    3. A plan of action that will move forward on a long-range basis to take full advantage of existing strengths and to provide changes to correct deficiencies.

Self-evaluation is an essential part of any improvement program but self-evaluation alone is not sufficient. A broad evaluative program should bring evaluators from outside the school who can examine the situation in a more objective manner. The internal and external evaluations must then be brought together and carefully studied, and a plan developed to proceed with an improvement program.

Evaluation is essential to any enterprise and the junior high school is no exception. The patrons of the school demand an evaluation of the individual pupil and the teacher usually accepts this responsibil-

---

[4] Oklahoma Curriculum Improvement Commission, *A Manual of Evaluation for the Junior High School* (Oklahoma City, Okla.: State Department of Education, 1958).

[5] William G. Anderson, "The Development and Trial of an Instrument for the Self-Evaluation of Junior High Schools, *Bulletin of the National Association of Secondary School Principals,* Vol. 46, No. 271 (February, 1962), 335–36.

ity. It seems logical that the program itself should be evaluated as continuously and as thoroughly as are the pupils who participate in it. It might be that many times poor personal evaluations of the pupils are a result of a poor program rather than of the performances of the pupils themselves.

CHAPTER XI

The Junior High School
Today and Tomorrow

Today's junior high school emerged from a downward extension of the senior high school. The original concept was aimed at starting a full-fledged secondary education at an earlier age, but the very nature of the boys and girls in Grades 7 and 8 resulted in a modification of the earlier ideas. Gradually the school has come to find itself in a unique role that is neither that of the elementary school nor that of the senior high school. In reality it is a transitional school designed to bridge the gap between the elementary and secondary schools.

The early idea of extending the secondary school downward was based strictly upon a subject matter-oriented concept that give little attention to the physical, psychological, and social needs of the age group to be served. It was recognized that the child of this age could do the work in the academic fields, but other aspects of the program demanded a different atmosphere for more effective learning. There has since been a shift toward a more suitable atmosphere but the change has been slow and too often we find the junior high school operating on the same basis as a senior high school. The effective junior high school program is a unique combination of both the elementary school and the senior high school programs—but with its own distinct personality that distinguishes it from both the schools from which it was taken.

The basic skills emphasis of the elementary school is continued through Grade 9, while the subject matter emphasis of the senior high school has been moved downward to include Grade 7. One of the basic problems of the junior high school concerns fusing these two approaches into a single effort that helps the child move gradually from one approach to the other. Some junior high schools are accomplishing this today, but others are oriented toward the senior high school point of view while a few still cling to the ideas of the conventional elementary school. Only time and work will bring about a school that takes the role of a true transitional school that gradually brings the child from one extreme of organization to the other.

The newness of the junior high school is one of its major disadvantages. The real function of the school is not fully understood by the public and very often it is not understood by the teachers who are responsible for the classroom program. It is not uncommon to find schools that move a course of instruction from the tenth grade to the ninth grade without making any adjustments in it. Much of the content from senior high school subject matter areas could be profitably taught in the junior high school, but not in its present form.

The generalized courses that have emerged in the curriculum of the junior high school are evidence of the move toward bringing the traditional subjects of the secondary school into the junior high school. General science and the general approach of modern mathematics are examples of this trend. Physics and chemistry courses in Grades 7, 8, and 9 would meet with difficulties, but many of the basic concepts of these sciences can be taught in the general courses of the junior high school and with this background the pupils can start at a much higher level when they reach the senior high school. The same is true for geometry and trigonometry. The generalized mathematics program of the junior high school can develop many of the algebraic, geometric, and trigonometric concepts, besides strengthening the basic arithmetic skills.

The lack of teacher education programs designed specifically for the junior high school is another factor that reflects the newness of the school. Colleges and universities have little demand for junior high school education because the unique position of the school is not yet recognized. Most of our elementary school teachers have had specific preparation for their work. The same is true for senior high school teachers. The junior high school offers a different picture: few of the teachers in today's junior high schools started their professional education with junior high school teaching as their goal. The result is that a large percentage of our junior high school teachers have had no special preparation. The insecurity of this situation has caused an instability in the school as evidenced by the turnover in the junior high school teaching staff—a turnover larger than that found in either the elementary school or in the senior high school.

In spite of the difficulties involved in the junior high school, the school is in a better position to capitalize on educational innovations than either the elementary or senior high school. Very often the most successful practices developed in the elementary school are difficult to adapt to the senior high school. The same is true for innovations developed in the senior high school that are not completely adaptable to the elementary situation. The junior high school is in a position to borrow from both levels and to adapt the new practices to its own situation. For example, the concept of team teaching in the senior high school has even better possibilities in the junior high school. The elementary school has one of the best ways yet developed for reporting pupil progress: parent-teacher conferences. With some modification, this idea can easily be adapted to the junior high school and become a most effective addition to the school.

Today's junior high school is establishing a definite pattern for a unique role in American education. The functions of the school are fairly well defined, but not yet fully understood and accepted. Many of these problems will disappear with the time that is required for any new institution to find its place in society. There is as much a need for a school to serve the period of transition for the adolescent as there is for an elementary school to serve the pre-adolescent and for the high school to serve the late adolescent. The existing design for the school is sound and more and more successful junior high school programs are being recognized by the public. The junior high school has found its place in the American system of education, but it will take some time for it to reach the level of maturity that will bring the recognition necessary for real success.

Bibliography

Conant, James B., *The American High School Today*. New York: McGraw-Hill Book Company, Inc., 1959.

———, *Education in the Junior High School Years*. Princeton, New Jersey: Educational Testing Service, 1960.

Faunce, Roland C. and Morrel J. Clute, *Teaching and Learning in the Junior High School*. Belmont, Calif.: Wadsworth Publishing Company, Inc., 1961.

Faunce, Roland C. and Nelson L. Bossing, *Developing the Core Curriculum*, 2nd ed. Englewood Cliffs, N.J.: Prentice-Hall, Inc., 1958.

Gaumnitz, Walter G., *Strengths and Weaknesses of the Junior High School*. Washington, D.C.: U. S. Department of Health, Education, and Welfare, 1955. (Report of the National Conference on Junior High Schools—1955.)

Grambs, Jean D., Clarence G. Noyce, Franklin Patterson and John Robertson, *The Junior High School We Need*. Washington, D.C.: Association for Supervision and Curriculum Development, 1961.

Gruhn, William T. and Harl R. Douglass, *The Modern Junior High School*, 2nd ed. New York: The Ronald Press Company, 1947.

Halfaker, Philip, *Trends in Junior High Schools*. Muncie, Indiana: Indiana Public School Study Council, 1961.

Iowa State Department of Public Instruction, *Junior High Schools for Iowa Youth*. Des Moines, Iowa: State of Iowa, 1960.

Koos, Leonard V., *Junior High School Trends*. New York: Harper & Row, Publishers, 1955.

Morphet, Edgar L., R. L. Johns, and Theodore L. Reller, *Educational Administration—Concepts, Practices, and Issues*. Englewood Cliffs, N.J.: Prentice-Hall, Inc., 1959.

National Association of Secondary-School Principals, "The Junior High School Idea in Theory and Practice," *The Bulletin of the National Association of Secondary-School Principals*, Vol. 46, No. 276 (October, 1962).

———, "Junior High-School Development, Practices and Research," *The Bulletin of the National Association of Secondary-School Principals*, Vol. 46, No. 271 (February, 1962).

———, "The Junior High-School Today and Tomorrow," *The Bulletin of the National Association of Secondary-School Principals*, Vol. 44, No. 259 (November, 1960).

Noar, Gertrude, *The Junior High School—Today and Tomorrow*. Englewood Cliffs, N.J.: Prentice-Hall, Inc., 1961.

Oklahoma Curriculum Improvement Commission, *A Manual of Evaluation for Junior High Schools*. Oklahoma City: Oklahoma State Department of Public Instruction, 1958.

Trump, J. Lloyd and Dorsey Baynham, *A Guide to Better Schools*. Chicago: Rand-McNally & Company, 1961.

Utah State Board of Education, *Junior High School Evaluative Criteria*. Salt Lake City: State of Utah, Department of Public Instruction, 1960.

Van Til, William, Gordon F. Vars, and John H. Lounsbury, *Modern Education for the Junior High School Years*. New York: The Bobbs-Merrill Company, Inc., 1961.

Wright, Grace S., *State Policies and Regulations Affecting the Junior High School*. Washington, D.C.: U. S. Department of Health, Education, and Welfare, 1955.

Index